ISAAVAASYA UPANISHAT

SANKARA, RAMAANUJEEYA AND

MADHWA COMMENTARIES

BY

RAVINDRANATH KADLABAL

pencil

ISBN 978-93-5458-679-8

Published in India 2021 by Pencil

A brand of

One Point Six Technologies Pvt. Ltd.

123, Building J2, Shram Seva Premises,

Wadala Truck Terminal, Wadala (E)

Mumbai 400037, Maharashtra, INDIA

E connect@thepencilapp.com

W www.thepencilapp.com

Author biography

Ravindranath Kadlabal is a post graduate in Sanskrit and a gradulate in Law. He has been an ardent student of Hindu Philosophy in general and Madhwa Philosophy in particular. He has retired as an Asst. General Manager in a Public Sector Bank. He has studied Isaavasya Upanishat under the guidance of Late Sri. A S Bheemasenachar during the year 1983. However, he has been studying the philosophical texts under the revered guruji Sri. Korlahalli Narasimhachar.

Ravindranath Kadlabal also teaches Bhagavadgita and other texts on a daily basis to around 10 to 15 persons with some week-end classes as well on other topics like Tarka.

Ravindranath Kadlabal has authored a book "Brahma Sutras - An Introduction through Anubhaashya of Sri. Madhwaachaarya" published by Poornaprajna Samshodhana Trust.

Contents

Introduction

॥ श्रीः ॥आसीनस्य शयानस्य तिष्टतो व्रजतोऽपि वा ।

रमस्व पुण्डरीकाक्ष हृदये मम सर्वदा ॥

Sankaraacharya : Sri Sankaraacharya provides a brief introduction to the Upanishat before he proceeds to interpret themantras.

ईशिता सर्वभूतानां सर्वभूतमयश्च यः ।

ईशावश्येन सम्बोध्यमीश्वरं तं नमाम्यहम् ॥

I pray him, the one who is addressed as *isaavashya* , the lord of everything and is himself everything. ईशा वास्यमित्यादयो मन्त्राः कर्मस्वनियुक्ताः । तेषामकर्मशेषस्यात्मनो याथात्म्य-प्रकाशकत्वात् । याथात्म्यं चात्मनः शुद्धत्वापापविद्धत्वैकत्वनित्यत्वाशरीरत्व सर्वगतत्वादिवक्ष्यमाणम् । तच्च कर्मणा विरुद्ध्येतेति युक्तः एवैषां कर्मस्वनियोगः । न ह्येवंलक्षणमात्मनो याथात्म्यमुत्पाद्यं विकार्यमाप्यं संस्कार्यं कर्तभोक्तृरूपं वा येन कर्मशेषता स्यात् । सर्वासामुपनिषदामात्म-याथात्म्यनिरूपणेनैवोपक्षयात् गीतानां मोक्षधर्माणां चैवम्परत्वात् । तस्मादात्मनोऽनेकत्व कर्तृत्व भोक्तृत्वादि चाशुद्धत्वपापविद्धत्वादि चौपादाय लोकबुद्धिसिद्ध कर्माणि विहितानि । This Upanishat does not preach *Karma* , the performance of duties but explains the nature of God. It describes God as unqualified, sinless, single, eternal, formless, omnipresent entity and this contradicts the karma theory. Hence this upanishat does not preach karma. God of above nature cannot be thought of as getting born, metamorphosing, acquiring, refining and getting subjected to performance of duties and entitlement to or enjoyment of its fruits in reality. Had it been so, he would have had the binding of *karma* . Hence all upanishats do preach only the aforesaid qualities of God. Even Bhagavad Geeta and *Moksha Dharma* texts also explain the aforesaid real nature of God. Hence the *Karma* path is prescribed for those who think of multiplicity of *jeevas* (soul / spirit), their capability to perform tasks, eligibility for their fruits, impurity, sins etc. Essentially, *karma* path is for those who cannot conceive the monoistic principles as explained above. यो हि कर्मफलेनार्थी दृष्टेन ब्रह्मवर्चसादिनादृष्टेन स्वर्गादिना च द्विजातिरहं न काणकुब्जत्वाद्यनधिकार प्रयोजकधर्मवानित्यात्मानं मन्यते सोऽधिक्रियते कर्मस्विति ह्यधिकारविदो वदन्ति ।

The wise, who know the eligibility criteria say that theone

- who has a desire for the visible benefits of *Karma* like *Brahma Tejas* (The prowess derived out of leading a life as per the scriptures) or
- who has a desire for the invisible benefits like swarga, the intermediary heaven and
- who is a dwija (one who has been initiated to veda) with no disabilities like blindness or dwarfness

is eligible for the path of *Karma* तस्मादेते मन्त्रा आत्मनो याथात्म्यप्रकाशनेन आत्मविषयं स्वाभाविकमज्ञानं निवर्तयन्त: शोकमोहादि संसारधर्मविच्छित्तिसाधनमात्मैकत्वादिविज्ञानमुत्पाद यन्ति । इत्येवमुक्ता-धिकार्यभिधेयसंबन्धप्रयोजनान्मन्त्रान्संक्षेपतो व्याख्यास्यामः । This upanishat presents the true picture of God, thereby removing the natural *ajnaana* , (ignorance) thereby causing the destruction of *sansaara* (the cycle of births and deaths), which is characterized by sorrow and illusion and bestows the knowledge of oneness of God with everything. After thus explaining *adhikaari, abhidheya, sambhandha and prayojana* of this Upanishat, we offer our interpretation to these mantraas as under: [Every book should essentially have four components viz., adhikaari (Target audience), viShaya (subject matter – also termed as abhidheya), sambandha (their inter-se relationship) and prayojana (benefit). The above introduction briefly explains these four components].

Raamaanujeeya : Since Bhashya of Sri Ramanujaacharya is not available, the commentary written by a follower of Sri Ramanujaacharya, by name Sri.

Narayana is taken here to present the Visishistaadvaita version of interpretation.

अथ वाजसनेयिनां संहितान्तिमाध्यायो व्याख्यायते-

सर्वेशानः सर्वभूतान्तरात्मा दोषानर्हः सर्वविद्येकवेद्यः ।
कर्माराध्यः साध्यभक्त्यैकलभ्यः श्रीमान्व्यक्तो वाजिनां संहितान्ते ॥

रजस्तमःप्रचुरकरणकलेवरसृष्टिविशिष्टत्वादीश्वरोऽहमहं भोगीत्यादिभगवदुक्तप्रक्रियया स्वतन्त्रोऽहं देवतान्तरपरतन्त्रोऽहमिति च भ्राम्यतस्तत्त्वबुभुत्सयोपसन्नस्य शिष्यस्य स्वतन्त्रतात्मभ्रमादिनिवृत्यर्थं चिदचिदात्मकस्य प्रपञ्चस्य परमपुरुषायत्तस्वरूप-स्थितिप्रवृत्तित्वमुपदिशति -

Following is the commentary on the last section of Vajasaneya samhita. Prayer: One who is the lord of everything, dwells in everyone, has absolutely no defect or deficiency, one who is described by the entire of vedas, one who is worshiped through performance of ordained duties, one who is available for only his devotees, is described in the last chapter of *Vajasaneya samhita.* Since most part of these physical bodies are made of rajas and tamas, the two of three basic elements, every individual feels "I am the lord, I deserve all the pleasures" etc., as told by lord Krishna in Bhagavad Geeta. Under the illusion of himself being independent or that he is being regulated by some other deity other than Narayana, he seeks to know the truth and approaches a Guru. With an intent to remove the illusion of such a disciple, the Guru preaches him the facts about the entire of this universe, that is made of chit (living) and achit (non-living) objects with no exception, that exists and remains active only because of the super personality, God.

Madwaacharya : Sri Madhwaacharya has a unique style of providing interpretation through quotations from various scripts. The quotes are so apt that in most of the cases, they adequately explain the inherent meaning of the Upanishat without a need for any further explanation.

नित्यानित्यजगद्धात्रे नित्याय ज्ञानमूर्तये ।
पूर्णानन्दाय हरये सर्वयज्ञभुजे नमः ॥

यस्मादब्रह्मेन्द्ररुदादिदेवतानां श्रियोऽपि च ।
ज्ञानस्फूर्तिस्सदा तस्मै हरये गुरवे नमः ॥

Prayer: Salutations to Hari who is the guardian of the entire universe comprising of eternal and transient objects, is himself eternal in absolute terms, an embodiment of knowledge, is full with pleasure and who is the recipient of the benefits of all yajnas. Salutations to Hari who is the source of knowledge for all the deities right from Brahma and Rudra and also for goddess Lakshmi and who is my Guru as well.

स्वायम्भुवो मनुरेतैर्मन्त्रैर्भगवन्तमाकूतिसूनुं यज्ञनामानं विष्णु तुष्टाव ।

Swaayambhuva manu prayed Vishnu who had incarnated himself in the name ' *Yajna* '. *Yajna* is the son of *Aakooti* , daughter of *Swaayambhuva* . *Swaayambhuva* prayed God, who was his grandson, with these mantras. Thus speaks *Brahmaanda puraana* :

स्वायम्भुवस्वदौहित्रं विष्णु यज्ञाभिधं मनुः ।
ईशावास्यादिभिर्मन्त्रैस्तुष्टावाऽवहितात्मना ।
रक्षोभिरुग्रैस्सम्प्राप्तः खादितुं मोचितस्तदा ।
स्तोत्रम् श्रुत्वैव यज्ञेन तान्हत्वाऽवध्यतां गतान् ॥
प्रादाद्धि भगवांस्तेषामवध्यत्वं हरः प्रभुः ।
तैर्वध्यत्वं तथान्येषामितः कोऽन्यो हरेः प्रभुः ॥

इति ब्रह्माण्डे

Manu (the person who starts the worldly creation) by name *Swaayambhuva* was attacked by the cruel demons with an intent to eat him up. He then, with an unperturbed mind prayed his daughter's (*Aakooti* 's) son by name *Yajna* with these mantras. *Yajna* is the incarnation of the supreme God *Vishnu* also known as *Hari* . These demons had a boon of immortality from Lord *Hara* (*Rudra*). Hence no one was capable of destroying those demons except lord *Hari* . *Yajna* , the incarnation of *Hari* rescued swaayambhuva and killed those dreaded demons.

भागवते चायमेवार्थ उक्तः ।

Even *Bhaagavata puraana* speaks of the same. (The name of the discoverer, presiding deity etc are also mentioned there).

UPANISHAT

ईशावास्यमिदं सर्वं

ईशावास्यमिदं सर्वं यत्किञ्च जगत्यां जगत् ।

तेन त्यक्तेन भुञ्जीथ मा गृधः कस्यस्विद्धनम् ॥ १॥

eesaavaasyam-idam sarvam

yatkincha jagatyaam jagat |

tena tyaktena bhunjeetha maa

gridah kasyasvid-dhanam |1|

Sankaraacharya : ईशा ईष्टे इति ईट्, तेन ईशा। ईशिता परमेश्वरः परमात्मा सर्वस्य। स हि सर्वमीष्टे सर्वजन्तूनामात्मा सन् प्रत्यगात्मतया । तेन स्वेन रूपेणात्मना ईशा वास्यम् आच्छादनीयम्।

The word " *eeSa* " is derived from the root "' *eeT* " meaning the one who rules. God is the ruler of everything. He is the soul of every being. He is there in every being as *pratyagaatma* (the inner one) and externally he wraps everything. (The word *eeSaavaasyam* is split as *eeSa* and *vaasyam* . Thus the word coveys the meaning that God covers / wrapseverything).

किम् ? इदं सर्वं यत्किं च यत्किञ्चित् जगत्यां पृथिव्यां जगत् तत्सर्वम् । स्वेनात्मना ईशेन प्रत्यगात्मतया अहमेवेदं सर्वमिति परमार्थसत्य-रूपेणानृतमिदं सर्वं चराचरमाच्छादनीयं परमात्मना । यथा चन्दनागर्वादेरुदकादिसम्बन्धजक्लेदादिजमौपाधिकं दौर्गन्ध्यं तत्स्वरूपनिघर्षणेनाच्छाद्यते स्वेन पारमार्थिकेन गन्धेन, तद्वदेव हि स्वात्मन्यध्यस्तं स्वाभाविकं कर्तृत्वभोक्तृत्वादिलक्षणं जगद्द्वैतरूपं पृथिव्याम्, जगत्यामित्युपलक्षणार्थ-त्वात्सर्वमेव नामरूपकर्माख्यं विकारजातं परमार्थसत्यात्मभावनया त्यक्तं स्यात्।

What all is wrapped? Everything. God, who is the ultimate truth and dwells inside everything, with a sense of such everything being himself, covers this fallacious everything, mobile or immobile. The way, perfume mixed in water covers the badly smelling particles existing in water with its fragrance and removes the bad odor, God covers the natural sense of *kartritva* and *bhokritva* (owning up the deeds and the enjoyment of their fruits) in every being by any name, shape (object) or action displaying multiplicity and removes those feelings for good with the sense of oneness with God.

एवमीश्वरात्मभावनया युक्तस्य पुत्राद्येषणात्रयसंन्यासे एवाधिकारः, न कर्मसु । तेन त्यक्तेन त्यागेनेत्यर्थः । न हि त्यक्तो मृतः पुत्रो भृत्यो वा आत्मसम्बन्धिताभावादात्मानं पालयति । अतस्त्यागेनेत्ययमेवार्थः । भुञ्जीथाः पालयेथाः । एवं त्यक्तैषणस्त्वं मा गृधः गृधिम् आकाङ्क्षां मा कार्षीः धनविषयाम् । कस्य स्वित् कस्यचित् परस्य स्वस्य वा धनं मा काङ्क्षीरित्यर्थः । स्विदित्यनर्थको निपातः ।

Thus the one who has the feeling of oneness with God is qualified for the renunciation of worldly desires of son, wife, wealth etc and not for *karma* (the performance of duties). A deserted son or servant will not serve the person deserting them. Hence, the word " *tyaaga* " (renunciation) is used in this sense by the upanishat. The word " *bhunjeethaah* " (enjoy) should be interpreted to mean " *paalayethaa* " (possessed). Thus having renounced the worldly desires, do not crave for wealth be it yours or of others. " *swit* " is a meaningless expression.

अथवा, मा गृधः । कस्मात् ? कस्य स्विद्धनम् इत्याक्षेपार्थः । न कस्यचिद्धनमस्ति, यद्गृध्येत । आत्मैवेदं सर्वमितीश्वरभावनया सर्वं त्यक्तम् । अत आत्मन एवेदं सर्वम् , आत्मैव च सर्वम् । अतो मिथ्याविषयां गृधिं मा कार्षीरित्यर्थः ॥

In other words, do not desire. Why? Because, there is nothing like other's wealth that can be craved for. Once you understand the oneness of everything with God and renounce everything as illusion, there is nothing left for desire.

Raamaanujeeya : इदं ब्रह्मादिस्तम्बपर्यन्तं सर्वमीश्वरव्यतिरिक्तं भोक्तृभोग्यरूपम् । ईशा सर्वनियन्त्रा पुरुषेणेति यावत् । "योऽसावसौ पुरुषः" इत्यनुवदिष्यमाणत्वात् । स हि सर्वस्येष्टे । तथा च श्रुत्यन्तरम् -"पतिं विश्वस्याऽऽत्मेश्वरम् (म ना० १२ । ३)" इति । तेन वास्यं वसनीयं व्याप्यमिति भावः । यच्च किंचिज्जगत्सर्वं दृश्यते श्रूयतेऽपि वा । अन्तर्बहिश्च तत्सर्वं व्याप्य

नारायणः स्थितः । (म ना०१११६) इति श्रुतेः । यद्वा सर्वाधारे स्वस्मिन्नेव सर्वं वास्यं प्रतिष्ठापनीयम् ।

स्मर्यतेहि-

सर्वत्रासौ समस्तं च वसत्यत्रेति वै यतः ।
ततः स वासुदेवेति विद्वद्भिः परिपठ्यते ॥ इति ॥

The entire of this universe, with the exception of God, comprising of *bhogya* - objects of enjoyment and *bhoktr* - the persons who enjoy is regulated by *purusha* . God who is referred to as isa here, is also called as *purusha* in this upanishat - " *yo asau asau purushah* " - He alone is the lord of everthing. *Mahanaarayana Upanishat* also speaks so - " *patim vishwasya aatmeshvaram* ". " *isaa vaasyam* " means that which is covered by eesa – the lord. So speaks *Mahanaarayana Upanishat* – whatever is seen or heard, whether stays inside or outside, everything of it is covered by (under the control of) *Naaraayana*.

Alternatively, the above mantra can mean, everything has to stay in this person who supports everything. So says the scripts – Since everything at everyplace stays in him, he is called *Vaasudeva* by the learned people.

जगत्यां मह्याम् । इदं लोकान्तरोपलक्षणम् । जगदन्यथात्वं गच्छत् । तत्राचिदंशस्य भोग्यत्वाय स्वरूपविकाररूपमन्यथात्वम् । चिदंशस्य तु भोक्तृत्वाय ज्ञानसंकोचविकासादिस्वभावविकारेण अन्यथात्वमिति भेदोऽनुसंधेयः । ईशेनावास्यं किंचिदपि नास्तीति दृढयितुं यत्किञ्चेति जगद्विशेष्यते । जगत्यादिषु लोकेषु यत्किञ्चिद्भोक्तृभोग्यरूपं जगदस्ति तदिदं सर्वमीशा वासुदेवेन वास्यं धार्यं चेति वाक्यार्थः ।

The word " *jagat* " though means the earthly world, it symbolically represents other worlds as well. All the *jada* objects are meant for use and hence are subject to changes. The *chit* objects (living ones – *jeevas*) experience modifications only in the form of a constriction or expansion of their knowledge but not materially. The words " *yat kinchit* ", meaning "anything and everything" are used to assert the fact that there is nothing which is not covered by eesa.

Thus, the mantra states that everything, be it jada or *chetana* , is covered by vaasudeva.

इन्द्रियाणि मनो बुद्धिः सत्त्वं तेजो बलं धृतिः।
वासुदेवात्मकान्याहुः क्षेत्रं क्षेत्रज्ञ एव च ॥ (गी० ३।४०)

इत्याद्युपबृंहणानि बोध्यानि "पृथगात्मानं प्रेरितारं च मत्वा (श्वे.उ.१६)। ज्ञाज्ञौ द्वावजा-वीशानीशौ" (श्वे.उ. .१९)। "नित्यो नित्यानां चेतन-श्चेतनानामेको बहूनां यो विदधाति कामान्" (श्वे.उ. ६१३) इत्यादिषु श्रुतिषु प्रसिद्धो जीवेश्वरयोरीशेशितव्यादिलक्षणोऽत्य-न्तभेदोऽप्यत्र सिद्धः । ननु रूढिर्योगमपहरतीति न्यायादीशोऽत्र रुद्रः स्यात्। मैवम्।

Bhagavad Geeta also supports this meaning that everything, be it the senses, mind, the intelligence, *satva* (the state of existence), the energy, strength, courage, physical body and jeeva, is under the control of *Vaasudeva* . Another upanishat says "The one who stimulates and the one subjected to it (*jeeva*) are different – one is full of knowledge and the other ignorant, both are eternal in existence, one is omnipotent and the other has meagre capabilities", "God is eternal amongst eternals, *chetana* amongst *chetanas* . He is the one amongst many and provides the desired benefits". These and other such statements clearly define the difference between *jeeva* and *eesa* (God). The rules of interpretation of vedas place *roodhi* (the popularity of usage) over the *yoga* (literal meaning) in priority. Thus the word *eesa* which is popular in deity *Rudra* should have meant him. However, it is not so because -

एको ह वै नारायण आसीन्न ब्रह्मा नेशानो नेमे द्यावापृथिवी न नक्षत्राणि न यमो नाग्निर्न सोमो न सूर्यः स एकाकी नर एव (म.उ.१)। इत्यादिषु श्रुतिषु भगवत्कार्यत्वेन कर्मवश्यत्वेन च संप्रतिपन्ने रुद्रे सर्वव्यापित्वसर्वाधारत्वादेरन्वयासंभवेन विरुद्धार्थविषयतयैव रूढेर्भग्नत्वात्। एवं च जगत्का

रणवादिवाक्यावगताकाशप्राणादि-शब्दन्यायेनाजः सर्वेश्वरः सिद्ध इत्यनवच्छिन्नैश्वर्यतया प्रसिद्धेः सर्वेश्वरेऽयोगिक एवायमीशशब्दः प्रत्येतव्य इति सिद्धम् ।

Mahanarayana Upanishat says " *Narayana* alone existed, neither *Brahma* , nor *Eesaana* , nor the deities of heaven, earth, stars, death, fire, moon or sun. He alone existed". Thus *Rudra* , who is created by God and stays under his control cannot be considered as omnipresent and guardian of all. Hence we cannot just rely on the usage to mean the word " *eesa* " as Rudra. This apart, the word isa has to be understood to mean Naarayana only based on the same principles of attributing such meaning to the words " *aakaasha* ", " *praana* " etc when they are spelt in the context of being universal creator. It is not just the yogic meaning that makes isa refer to Naarayana but also the usage as in " *ajah sarveshvarah siddhah* ".

एवं मुमुक्षोरीश्वरपारतन्त्र्यबोधमुत्पाद्य वैराग्यभूषितां वृत्तिमुपदिशति - तेन त्यक्तेन भुञ्जीथाः । तेन जगता भोग्यताभ्रमविषयेणेति भावः । त्यक्तेनाल्पत्वास्थिरत्वदुःखमूलत्वदुःखमिश्रत्व-दुःखोदर्कत्वदेहाभिमानमूलत्वादिस्वाभाविकब्रह्मानन्दानुभवविरुद्धरूपविषयदोषनिरूपणपूर्वकपरित्यक्तेनोपलक्षितः सन्भुञ्जीथाः । भगवदुपासोपयुक्तदेहस्य धारणमात्रौपयिकमन्नपानादिकं यागदान-होमार्चनाद्युपयोगिपरिजन-परिच्छदादिकं च वर्गं भुञ्जीथा इत्यर्थः । यद्वा दोषसप्तकनिरूप-णात्त्यक्तेन भोग्याभासेनोपलक्षितः सन्भुञ्जीथाः । सर्वावासत्वेन प्रकरणप्राप्तं प्रकृतमुक्तदोषप्रतिभटं निरतिशयभोग्यं वक्ष्यमाणोपायमूढेन भुञ्जीथा इति योज्यम् ।

After thus explaining the dependence of *jeeva* on God, the upanishat now preaches the need for *karma* backed by *vairaagya* (the absence of desire for material pleasures). This is possible when one understands the defects of this world which is (i) silly, (ii) short lived, (iii) caused by sorrow, (iv) mixed with pains, (v) cause of future sorrow, (vi) caused out of the sense of "mine" in this physical body etc and (vii) an obstacle to the enjoyment of natural divine pleasure. This body is meant for *upaasana* of God and it should be fed with only food and water that is limited to and essential for its healthy survival and for the protection of those around us who support our performance of yaaga, daana (donation), homa, archana etc.

This also means that one should enjoy the objects after having known the aforesaid seven defects.

In effect, the mantra means that by understanding God as occupying everything and that everything is having the listed defects, one should consume only what is essential, in the way it is explained in the subsequent mantras of this upanishat.

तत्र "भोक्ता भोग्यं प्रेरितारं च मत्वा" (श्वे.उ.१।१२) "द्वा सुपर्णा सयुजा सखाया समानं वृक्षं परिपस्वजाते। तयोरन्यः पिप्पलं स्वाद्वत्त्यनश्नन्नन्यो अभिचाकशीति" (मुण्ड.उ.३।१) "समाने वृक्षे पुरुषो निमग्नोऽनीशया शोचति मुह्यमानः। जुष्टं यदा पश्यत्यन्य-मीशमस्य महिमानमिति वीतशोकः" (मु.उ.३।,२) इत्यादिभिः प्रपञ्चितस्तत्त्वत्रयविवेकोऽप्यत्रेति भावः । अनीशया भोग्यभूतया मायया प्रकृत्येत्यर्थः । जुष्टं प्रीयमाणम् । स्वस्मादन्यमीशमस्येशस्य महिमानमिति महिमानं चेत्यर्थः । तदितिप्रतिनिर्देशोऽध्याहार्यः । यदाऽन्यमीशमस्य महिमानं च पश्यति तदा वीतशोको भवतीत्यर्थः ।

This mantra also indicates the distinct three objects – the consumer, the consumed and the enabler *(jeeva, prakriti and eesha)* as explained in the upanishadic texts like " *Jeeva* , having understood the distinction between the objects to be consumed and the motivator", "Two birds, both being friends and staying together and they both are staying on the same tree. Whilst one eats the fruits in full swing, the other shines without eating anything". "Though *Jeeva* stays along with God on the same tree, he suffers on account of *prakriti* . When he finds the other as lovable and knows his glory, he shreds all sorrow".

मा गृधः कस्यस्विद्धनम् । कस्यचिद्धनं कस्यापि बन्धोरबन्धोर्वा धनं मा गृधः, माऽभिकाङ्क्षीः । गृधु अभिकाङ्क्षायामितिधातुः ।

Do not yearn for wealth of some one, whether or not he is your relative.

आह च यमः किंकरंप्रति- परमसुहृदि बान्धवे कलत्रे सुतवनितापितृमातृभृत्यवर्गे।
शठमतिरुपयाति योऽर्थतृष्णां पुरुषपशुर्नहि वासुदेवभक्तः ॥

इति स्मृतेः।

इदं च धनाशाप्रहाणं परमात्मव्यतिरिक्तकृत्स्नविषयवैराग्योपलक्षणम् । परमात्मनि यो रक्तो विरक्तोऽपरमात्मनि। इति स्मृतेः ॥ १ ॥

Thus spoke deity *Yama* to his servants – in quest of money, when one approaches his close friends, relatives, wife, daughter-in-law, father, mother or the servants, such a fool is a pet animal of those who are thirsty of wealth and is never a devotee of *Vaasudeva* .

This criticism of desire for money explains the quality of *vairaagya* which would mean detachment with everything other than God. *Vairaagya* means an interest in God with dispassion in everything else.

Madhwaacharya : ईशस्यावासयोग्यमीशावास्यम्। जगत्यां प्रकृत्तौ। तेनेशेन त्यक्तेन दत्तेन भुञ्जीथाः ॥

That which deserves occupancy (*aavaasyam*) of God is *eeSaavaasyam* . The word *jagat* means " *prakriti* " the universe (not just the earth). Thus, we should enjoy whatever has been granted by God (i.e., we should be contented with whatever we get in the natural course – should not beg others). The word " *tyakta* " (discarded) should be understood as " *datta* " (given).

स्वत: प्रवृत्यशक्तत्वादीशावास्यमिदं जगत्।
प्रवृत्तये प्रकृतिगं यस्मात्स प्रकृतीश्वरः ॥
तदधीनप्रवृत्तित्वात्तदीयं सर्वमेव तत्।
तद्दत्तेनैव भुञ्जीथा अतो नान्यं प्रयाचयेत् ॥

Brahmanda purana says: The universe cannot act on its own. Hence God enters and energizes it. Since the entire universe acts under his control, everything of it belongs to him. Hence we should enjoy whatever is granted by him and should not beg others.

कुर्वन्नेवेह कर्माणि

कुर्वन्नेवेह कर्माणि जिजीविषेच्छत ँ समाः ।
एवं त्वयि नान्यथेतोऽस्ति न कर्म लिप्यते नरे ॥ २ ॥

kurvanneveha karmaaNi

jijeevishech-chathagm samaah |

evam twayi naanyathetosti na

karma lipyate nare |2|

<u>Sankaraachaarya</u> : एवमात्मविदः पुत्राद्येषणात्रयसंन्यासेनात्म-ज्ञाननिष्ठतया आत्मा रक्षितव्य इत्येष वेदार्थः । अथेतरस्य अनात्मज्ञ-तयात्मग्रहणाशक्तस्य इदमुपदिशति मन्त्रः-

The one who has known God will have to protect " *aatma* " through the renouncement of the most desired aspects like son and by staying firm in the knowledge of God. This is the intent of Veda. However, the following mantra is directed at such others who have not understood God and who are not capable of understanding oneness with God.

कुर्वन्नेव निर्वर्तयन्नेव इह कर्माणि अग्निहोत्रादीनि जिजीविषेत् जीवितुमिच्छेत् शतं शतसङ्ख्याकाः समाः संवत्सरान् । तावद्धि पुरुषस्य परमायुर्निरूपितम् । तथा च प्राप्तानुवादेन यज्जिजीविषेच्छतं वर्षाणि तत्कुर्वन्नेव कर्माणीत्येतद्विधीयते । एवम् एवंप्रकारे त्वयि जिजीविषति नरे नरमात्राभिमानिनि इतः एतस्मादग्निहोत्रादीनि कर्माणि कुर्वतो वर्तमानात्प्रकारात् अन्यथा प्रकारान्तरं नास्ति, येन प्रकारेणाशुभं कर्म न लिप्यते ; कर्मणा न लिप्यस इत्यर्थः । अतः शास्त्रविहितानि कर्माण्यग्निहोत्रादीनि कुर्वन्नेव जिजीविषेत् ॥

If you desire to live a hundred years, you can do so only if you keep doing the prescribed tasks like agnihotra. Hundred years is considered as the maximum life span of a person. Veda (upanishat) thus stipulates that any one who desires to live a hundred years, shall do so by performing the prescribed duties.

Thus for you the human, there is no way you live, other than through the performance of prescribed duties like agnihotra. With this alone, you can remain untainted by the evils of the bad deeds. Hence, you should desire to live only with the performance of duties like agnihotra as prescribed by the scriptures.

कथं पुनरिदमवगम्यते - पूर्वेण मन्त्रेण संन्यासिनो ज्ञाननिष्ठोक्ता, द्वितीयेन तदशक्तस्य कर्मनिष्ठेति ? उच्यते - ज्ञानकर्मणोर्विरोधं पर्वतवदकम्प्यं यथोक्तं न स्मरसि किम् ? इहाप्युक्तम् - यो हि जिजीविषेत्स कर्माणि कुर्वन्नेव इति ; 'ईशा वास्यमिदं सर्वम्', 'तेन त्यक्तेन भुञ्जीथाः मा गृधः कस्य स्विद्धनम्' इति च। 'न जीविते मरणे वा गृधिं कुर्वीतारण्यमियात् इति पदं ततो न पुनरेयात्' इति च संन्यासशासनात्। उभयोः फलभेदं च वक्ष्यति।

How then should we know that the first mantra is meant for jnaani (learned people), who can renounce the desires and the second is for those who cannot do so but are engaged in karma? Don't you remember that the difference between the two paths is rock stable? Even here it is said "He who desires to live shall do so by performance", "Everything is covered by God", "Hence live a renounced life", "Do not greed for other's wealth". There should be no greed either in life or in death. "Should go to woods and should not return" are the dicta for the renounced. The difference in effect of the two paths is also explained as under:

"इमौ द्वावेव पन्थानावनुनिष्क्रान्ततरौ भवतः क्रियापथश्चैव पुरस्तात्संन्यासश्च" ; तयोः संन्यास एवातिरेचयति - "न्यास एवात्यरेचयत्" (तै. नारा. ७८) इति तैत्तिरीयके।"

द्वाविमावथ पन्थानौ यत्र वेदाः प्रतिष्ठिताः।
प्रवृत्तिलक्षणो धर्मो निवृत्तिश्च विभाषितः" (मो. ध. २४१। ६)

इत्यादि पुत्राय विचार्य निश्चितमुक्तं व्यासेन वेदाचार्येण भगवता। विभागं चानयोः प्रदर्शयिष्यामः॥

There are only two paths right from the time of creation. The path of Karma on the one hand and the path of renunciation on the other. The later is through the detachment from the most desired things like son, wife etc. Of these, the path of renunciation is the supreme. Even Taittareeya text speaks of the same:

“There are two Vedic paths, the one that goes with worldly desires and the other excels with their renunciation”.

Lord Vyaasa, the principal teacher of Vedas has preached these definitive aspects to his son. We will further explain the difference between these paths in subsequent parts of this text.

Raamaanujeeya : एवं विरक्तस्य विदुषः फलसङ्गकर्तृत्वादिरहितो ब्रह्मविद्याङ्गभूतः कर्मयोगो यावज्जीवमनुष्ठेय इत्याह-

The following mantra says that the wise who has detached from result oriented tasks should perform karma yoga, which is part of brahma vidya, through out his life:

शतंसमाः, शतंसंवत्सरान्। कर्माणि नित्यनैमित्तिकानि। कुर्वन्नेवेह लोके जिजीविषेज्जीवितुमिच्छेत् । ब्रह्मविदोऽपि यावद्विद्यापूर्ति जीवितुमिच्छा भवतीति प्राप्तत्वात् । शतायुर्वै पुरुष इति श्रुतेः यावज्जीवं नित्यनैमित्तिककर्माणि कुर्वीतेति विधिः संक्रामयितव्यः । यावज्ज्ञानयोगाधिकारं कर्मयोगः कर्तव्य इति भावः । न कदाचिदपि विद्याङ्गं कर्म परित्यजेदित्येवकाराभिप्रायः । त्वयि। ईश्वरपरतन्त्र-रूपज्ञानतया तदाज्ञापरिपालनरूपकर्मानुष्ठानेऽधिकारप्रसिमतीति भावः । एवमेवानुष्ठानमित्यर्थः ।

One should desire to live a hundred years only by performing the prescribed daily (nitya) tasks and those prescribed as incidental to some event (naimittika). Even the one who has known God, should do it till such time his learning is complete and as long as he desires to live. The reference of hundred years is only with an estimate of standard span of life as told in the scripts that say “people live a hundred years”. The performance of tasks is not limited to hundred years but should continue as long as the desire to live exists. This karma yoga of performance of prescribed tasks should continue till such time one becomes eligible for jnaana yoga. It should never be discarded.

Thus, there is no choice for you, the one dependent on God and aware of it, but to perform the prescribed tasks that are nothing but dicta of God.

उक्तमर्थं व्यतिरेकेण दृढी करोति नान्यथेतोऽस्तीति । इतः कर्मानुष्ठानादन्यथा प्रकारान्तरं नास्तीत्यर्थः । नान्यः पन्थास्तत्तोषकारणमिति स्मृतेः।

The mantra asserts this meaning by telling the consequence of non-performance. There is no choice but to perform. Scripts say "there is no other way you can please God".

नन्वीश्वरवेदिनोऽपि कर्मानुष्ठानावश्यंभावी बन्धः स्यादित्याशङ्क्य आह - न कर्म लिप्यते नर इति । ब्रह्मविद्याविरुद्धेषु कर्मफलेषु "न रमत इति नरः" प्रस्तुतब्रह्मविदि नरे विद्याङ्गतया क्रियमाणं कर्म न लिप्यते न स्वर्गादिहेतुर्भवति प्रत्युत शुद्धप्रत्यगात्मसाक्षात्कारमेवो-त्पादयतीति भावः । यत्तु कुर्वन्नेवेह कर्माणीत्ययं विधिरविद्वद्विषय एष नतु बह्मविद्विषयस्तस्य विधिनिषेधशास्त्रवश्यत्वाभा वादिति व्याख्यानम् । तत्पकरणविरुद्धम् । 'विद्यां चाविद्यां च यस्तद्वेदोभयं सह' (ई.उ.।११) इत्याद्युपरितनविध्यन्तरविरुद्धं चेति न वेदविदो बहु मन्वते ॥ २॥

If everyone has to do karma, is it not that even a jnaani also would get bound by karma? No, such a person would not engage in the tasks that are against achieving brahma vidya (knowledge of God). The word "nara" in the mantra means "a person who does not enjoy" – one who would not enjoy karma that forms an obstacle in the achievement of brahma vidya. On the other hand, the tasks done by a brahma jnaani as part of vidya would not bind him to cause swarga, the temporary heaven etc but would support in getting saakshaatkaara (physical perception) of the pure form of God.

It is contrary to the "prakarana" (context of the chapter) to say "the mandate to perform karma relates only to the unwise but not to those who are wise, for the wise is beyond the religious prescriptions". Such an interpretation is also contrary to what is told in the subsequent mantra "vidyaam cha avidyaam cha" etc of this upanishat.

<u>Madhwaachaarya</u> : अकुर्वतः कर्म न लिप्यत इति नास्ति ।

It is never true that one does not get tainted with the fruits of karma if he refrains from the performance of prescribed duties.

अज्ञस्य कर्म लिप्येत कष्णोपास्तिमकुर्वतः ।
ज्ञानिनोऽपि यतो ह्रास आनन्दस्य भवेद्ध्रुवम् ।
अतोऽलेपेऽपि लेपस्स्यादत: कार्यैव सा सदा ॥ इति नारदीये

naarada purana says:

"It is certain that the ignorant (those who have not yet attained the enlightenment) get tainted with the results of karma if he does not worship Krishna. Even the enlightened (liberated) souls will have diminished pleasure if they do not do the ordained duties. Since the karma stains (if they fail in the performance of duties) even those who are normally immune to karma, one should always do the prescribed tasks".

असुर्या नाम ते

असुर्या नाम ते लोका अन्धेन तमसा वृताः ।

तांस्ते प्रेत्याभिगच्छन्ति ये के चात्महनो जनाः॥ ३ ॥

asuryaa naama te lokaa andhena tamasaavritaah |

taamste pretya-abhigacchanti ye ke chaatma-hano janaah |3|

Sanakaraacharya : अथेदानीमविद्वन्निन्दार्थोऽयं मन्त्र आरभ्यते-

असुर्याः परमात्मभावमद्वयमपेक्ष्य देवादयोऽप्यसुराः । तेषां च स्वभूता लोका असुर्याः नाम । नामशब्दोऽनर्थको निपातः ।

Now, this mantra proceeds to decry the unwise -

Everyone except *paramaatma*, God as conceived in monoism, including the deities (like *indra, varuna*) is " *asura* ". Their *loka* (world) is called " *asurya* ". The word " *naama* " is an useless expression.

ते लोकाः कर्मफलानि लोक्यन्ते दृश्यन्ते भुज्यन्त इति जन्मानि । अन्धेन अदर्शनात्मकेनाज्ञानेन तमसा आवृताः आच्छादिताः । तान् स्थावरान्तान्, प्रेत्य त्यक्त्वेमं देहम् अभिगच्छन्ति यथाकर्म यथाश्रुतम् । ये के च आत्महनः आत्मानं घ्नन्तीत्यात्महनः । के ? ते जनाः येऽविद्वांसः । कथं ते आत्मानं नित्यं हिंसन्ति ? अविद्यादोषेण विद्यमानस्यात्मनस्तिरस्करणात् । विद्यमानस्यात्मनो यत्कार्यं फलमजरामरत्वादि-संवेदनादिलक्षणम् , तत् हतस्येव तिरोभूतं भवतीति प्राकृता अविद्वांसो जना आत्महन इत्युच्यन्ते । तेन ह्यात्महननदोषेण संसरन्ति ते ॥

loka means births - those that are seen, that are enjoyed (or suffered) as fruits of our past deeds. These are engulfed in the darkness of ignorance that prevent vision. After exiting all such bodies (that he has been acquiring on account of *karma*), including the silliest of them, that of plants, jeeva would reach the places based on his *karma* and *jnaana* .

He who kills ' *aatma* ' (soul) is *aatmahana* . These are the ignorant people. Who are they? How can they kill an immortal *aatma* ? When an *aatma* ignores his self and identifies himself differently than what he really is on account of *avidya* (improper knowledge), the experience of true qualities like agelessness and immortality gets hidden. Hence, such a foolish person is called " *aatmahaa* ", the one who has destroyed himself. Such an individual moves in the cycle of births and deaths because of this defect.

Raamaanujeeya : एवं मन्त्रद्वयेन तत्त्वद्वयं विद्याङ्गकर्मानुष्ठानं चोपदिष्टम् । ईशनीय आसुरप्रकृतयः शास्त्रविधिमुत्सृज्य यज्ञादि कर्म कुर्वन्ति निषिद्धकर्म चाऽचरन्ति आत्मघातिनो निरयपातिन इत्युपदिशत्याचार्यः -

असुराणां स्वभूता असुर्या अतिदारुणा इत्यर्थः । नामेति प्रसिद्धौ । असुरस्वभावानुभाव्या निरयसंज्ञिता लोकाः सन्तीति शास्त्रप्रसिद्धमिति भावः । तान्विशिनष्टि - अन्धेन तमसाऽऽवृता इति । अन्धेनातिगाढेन तमसाऽन्धकारेणाऽऽवृता व्याप्ताः । आलोकप्रसङ्गरहिता इति भावः । ये केचन देवा मनुष्या ब्राह्मणक्षत्रियादयो वाऽऽत्महनः । 'असन्नेव स भवत्यसद्ब्रह्मेति वेद चेत्' । (तै.उ. २०६९।) इत्याम्नाता ब्रह्मज्ञानविहीनाः । काम्यनिषिद्धकर्मादिनिष्ठा इत्यर्थः । जना जनिमन्तः संसरन्त इत्यर्थः । ते प्रेत्य देहादुत्क्रम्य तानभितो गच्छन्ति । तान्पृथिव्यन्तरिक्षस्वर्गरौरवादिसंज्ञितान्निरयान्निरन्तरं गच्छन्तीति भावः ॥३॥

With the initial two mantras, two basic tatvas (*eesa* and *jeeva*) have been explained. Similarly, the concepts of karma as a component of knowledge is also explained. Now, the upanishat proceeds to speak of those *jeevas* who are of evil nature, perform *yajna* etc ignoring the rules set for them, perform tasks prohibited by the scripts, there by destroying themselves and fall in the eternal hells.

The word *asurya* means, that pertaining to *ausras* (evil minded people) – horrible places. These places are named *niraya* in scriptures, where the inherent nature of *asuras* is experienced. How are they? Filled with thick blinding darkness with no scope for light. Anyone, be he a human, deity, brahmana, kshatriya etc, who destroys himself would go to the aforesaid dark lands of tamas. *Taittareeya* upanishat says - those who believe in God as *asat* , non-existent, would become *asat* himself. Meaning, those who do not understand God properly, would perform materialistic tasks and get tied to this cycle of births and deaths.

Madhwaachaarya : सुष्टु रमणविरुद्धत्वादसुराणां प्राप्यत्वाच्चा-सुर्याः । "न च रमन्त्यहो असदुपासनयाऽऽत्महनः" इत्युक्तत्वात् ।Pure enjoyment is *suryam* . The place where there can be no enjoyment is *asurya* . There is only extreme sorrow in that place. This apart, *asurya* also means the destination of *asuras* (evil persons). Those who practice improper knowledge are deprived of enjoyment and hence are called *aatmahanah* . The soul is immortal and hence the word aatmahaa is not intended to mean its destruction. It only means begetting extreme sorrow coupled with the total absence of pleasure.

महादुःखैकहेतुत्वात् प्राप्यत्वादसुरैस्तथा ।
असुर्या नाम ते लोकास्तान्यान्ति विमुखा हरौ ।

इति च वामने ।

The world, where there is only extreme sorrow and happens to be the destination of *asuras* (evil souls) is called *asurya* . It is here where those who do not worship lord *Hari* land themselves up. - *Vaamana puraNa*

ये के चेति नियम उक्तः । "नियमेन तमो यान्ति सर्वेऽपि विमुखा हरौ" इति च ॥३॥

The expression "all those who" (ये के च) indicates the rule. Those who turn their backs to lord *Hari* will invariably land themselves up in the aforesaid dark world.

अनेजदेकं

अनेजदेकं मनसो जवीयो नैनद्देवा आप्नुवन् पूर्वमर्षत् ।

तद्धावतोऽन्यानत्येति तिष्ठत्तस्मिन्नपो मातरिश्वा दधाति ॥ ४ ॥

anejadekam manaso javeeyo nainaddeva aapnuvan poorvamarShat|

tad-dhaavato-nyaan atyeti tiShtatya-sminnapo maatariSva dadhaati|4|

Sankaraachaarya : यस्यात्मनो हननादविद्वांसः संसरन्ति, तद्वि-पर्ययेण विद्वांसो मुच्यन्तेऽनात्महनः, तत्कीदृशमात्मतत्त्वमित्युच्यते -

Who is this *aatma* , whose destruction by the ignorant causes *samsaara* (the cycle of births and deaths) and not doing so by the learned leads to achieving *moksha* ? This *aatma* is explained here.

अनेजत् न एजत् । "एजृ कम्पने", कम्पनं चलनं स्वावस्थाप्रच्युतिः, तद्वर्जितम् , सर्वदा एकरूपमित्यर्थः । तच्च एकं सर्वभूतेषु । मनसः सङ्कल्पादिलक्षणात् जवीयो जववत्तरम् ।

anejat means stable - immune to changes from the existing status. (Total absence of any change on account of time, growth, deterioration, acquisition, shredding etc). Thus it means an eternal stability in its form. There is only one and only one such thing and it is faster than the formation of thoughts in the mind.

कथं विरुद्धमुच्यते - ध्रुवं निश्चलमिदम्, मनसो जवीय इति च ? नैष दोषः, निरुपाध्युपाधिमत्त्वेनोपपत्तेः । तत्र निरुपाधिकेन स्वेन रूपेणोच्यते - अनेजदेकम् इति । मनसः अन्तःकरणस्य सङ्कल्प-विकल्पलक्षणस्योपाधेरनुवर्तनात् । इह देहस्थस्य मनसो ब्रह्मलोकादि-दूरस्थसङ्कल्पनं क्षणमात्राद्भवतीत्यतो मनसो जविष्ठत्वं लोक-प्रसिद्धम् । तस्मिन्मनसि ब्रह्मलोकादीन् द्रुतं गच्छति सति, प्रथमप्राप्त इवात्मचैतन्याभासो गृह्यते । अतः मनसो जवीयः इत्याह ।

Is it not contradictory to say that it is immobile but faster than mind? Not really. They fit in due to their contextual references. God is immobile in his original unassociated form whereas he is faster than thought on account of his association with the mind that is characterized by decision and dilemma.

Thought is considered to be the fastest on account of its reaching the farthest worlds like *brahma loka* the moment it is conceived, in a split second and it gets a feeling that God has already reached that place. Hence God is considered faster than mind.

नैनद्देवाः, द्योतनाद्देवाः चक्षुरादीनीन्द्रियाणि, एनत् प्रकृतमात्मतत्त्वं नाप्नुवन् न प्राप्तवन्तः। तेभ्यो मनो जवीयः। मनोव्यापारव्यवहित-त्वादाभासमात्रमप्यात्मनो नैव देवानां विषयीभवति ;

The deities are called *deva* because they illuminate (energize) the sense organs. These deities cannot reach God, aatma. The deity in charge of the mind discipline is the fastest amongst them. Even he cannot understand God. Since all perceptions happen through the co-ordination of mind, when mind itself cannot reach / understand God, God cannot be reached by any of these deities.

यस्माज्जवनान्मनसोऽपि पूर्वमर्षत् पूर्वमेव गतम् , व्योमवद्व्यापित्वात्। सर्वव्यापि तदात्मतत्त्वं सर्वसंसारधर्मवर्जितं स्वेन निरुपाधिकेन स्वरूपेणाविक्रियमेव सत् , उपाधिकृताः सर्वाः संसारविक्रिया अनुभवतीवाविवेकिनां मूढानामनेकमिव च प्रतिदेहं प्रत्यवभासत इत्येतदाह -

This *aatmatatva* God, is omnipresent like space. Hence he has been faster than the mind and thereby has reached every place before anyone could. This *aatmatatva* , God is devoid of all worldly attributes. He remains unvarying in his unattached form but is understood by the ignorant and foolish people, as subjected to changes of *samsaara* in his linked forms dwelling in every body. This is described as under:

तत् धावतः द्रुतं गच्छतः अन्यान् आत्मविलक्षणान्मनोवागिन्द्रियप्रभृतीन् अत्येति अतीत्य गच्छतीव। इवार्थं स्वयमेव दर्शयति - तिष्ठदिति, स्वयमविक्रियमेव सदित्यर्थः।

It looks like he surpasses all speeding things like mind, spoken words etc. The intent of the word " *iva* " meaning "like", is explained by the Upanishat itself with the word " *tishtat* " - he does so while he remains stable and immobile.

तस्मिन् आत्मतत्त्वे सति नित्यचैतन्यस्वभावे, मातरिश्वा मातरि अन्तरिक्षे श्वयति गच्छतीति मातरिश्वा वायुः सर्वप्राणभृत्क्रियात्मकः, यदाश्रयाणि कार्यकरणजातानि यस्मिन्नोतानि प्रोतानि च, यत्सूत्रसंज्ञकं सर्वस्य जगतो विधारयितृ, स मातरिश्वा, अपः कर्माणि प्राणिनां चेष्टालक्षणानि अग्न्यादित्यपर्जन्यादीनां ज्वलनदहनप्रकाशाभिवर्षणादिलक्षणानि, दधाति विभजतीत्यर्थः

While this *aatmatatva* God stays so, *Vaayu* , the deity of Air distributes the tasks of all beings. The tasks of heating, burning, illuminating, raining etc are distributed amongst agni, aaditya, parjanya etc. The word *maatarishva* means the one who moves in space (maatari). He is the one who is responsible for the life of every living being. He is the embodiment of activities. He enables all activity in the world. He stays in and out of all beings in the world and is their life support. Hence he is also called *sootra* the thread.

धारयतीति वा "भीषास्माद्वातः पवते" इत्यादिश्रुतिभ्यः । सर्वा हि कार्यकरणविक्रिया नित्यचैतन्यात्मस्वरूपे सर्वास्पदभूते सत्येव भवन्तीत्यर्थः ॥

The word *dadhaati* is meant as "distributes" above, it can also be understood to mean "he who bears" based on the Vedic expressions like "Scared of him, the wind blows" etc. Every change that happens as cause and effect, does so because of the action of God, the eternal embodiment of activity existing in every living being.

<u>Raamaanujeeya</u> :

एवं विद्यायां शीघ्रं प्रतिपत्तिसिद्ध्यर्थमविदुषामनर्थ उक्तः । अथ सर्वा-वासत्वेन प्रस्तुतस्येश्वरस्यानन्तविचित्रशक्तियोगं व्यञ्जयन्नुपदिशति -

Thus, having emphasized the need for a quick adoption of the path of knowledge by explaining the loss of those who do not follow it, the upanishat now explains the innumerable extraordinary capabilities of God who has been referred to as omnipresent in the earlier mantra.

अनेजन्न कम्पमानम् । एजृ कम्पने । एकं प्रधानतमम् । प्रधानं शास्त्रविदुषामिति रुद्रस्मृतेः । स्वाधिकसमानद्वितीयरहितमिति वा । "न तत्समश्चाभ्यधिकश्च दृश्यते" (श्वे.उ. ६।८।) इतिश्रुतेः । परमसाम्यमापन्ना अपि मुक्ता ईशाधीना एवेति भावः । मनसो जवीयः, वेगवतो मनसो जवीयो वेगवत्तरम् । निष्कम्पं वेगवत्तरं चेति विरोधः प्रतीयते । परिहारस्तु विभुत्वाद्वस्तुतो नैजति तत एव मनसो गोचरदेशे वर्तत इति मनसो जवीय इत्युपचर्यत इति । किंच देवा ब्रह्मरुद्रादयः पूर्वमर्षत् । प्रागेव सर्वान्देवान्प्राप्नुवन्नित्यर्थः । एतत्प्रस्तुतं सर्वावासं ब्रह्म नाऽऽप्नुवन्नेतावन्तं कालं न लेभिर इति भावः । पूर्वमेव प्राप्तं न प्राप्नुवन्निति च विरोधः । विभुतया प्राप्तमपि कर्मसंकुचितज्ञानाः क्षेत्रज्ञा आचार्योपदेशमन्तरेण स्वबुद्ध्या नाप्नुऽऽवन्तीति परिहारः । तथोक्तं छान्दोग्ये "तद्यथाऽपि हिरण्यनिधिं निहितमक्षेत्रज्ञा उपर्युपरि संचरन्तो न विन्देयुरेवमेवेमाः सर्वाः प्रजा अहरहर्गच्छन्त्य एतं ब्रह्मलोकं न विन्दन्त्यनृतेन हि प्रत्यूढाः (छा. उ. ८।३।२)" इति । "अपि तद्धावतोऽन्यानत्येति यः पृथिव्यां तिष्ठन्" (बृ.उ.३।७।३) "य आत्मनि तिष्ठन्" । "यः सर्वभूतेषु तिष्ठन्" इत्यादिश्रुतेः । सर्वत्र तिष्ठदेव तद्ब्रह्म धावतोऽन्यान्देवादीनत्येति । तिष्ठतः पुरुषस्य धावदतिक्रमणं न घटत इति विरोधः । जविनो यावद्यावद्धावन्ति तावतस्तावत: परस्तादपि वर्तत इति तात्पर्यादविरोधः । तस्मिन्नपो मातरिश्वा दधाति । तस्मिन्सर्वावासेऽवस्थितो मातरिश्वा वायुः । अप इत्युपलक्षणं पयोधरग्रहनक्षत्रतारकादिकं बिभर्तीत्यर्थः । सर्वाधारभूतेन सर्वेश्वरेण विधृतो वायुस्तत्सत्तयैव बिभर्तीत्यभिप्रायः । एष सेतुर्विधरण एषां लोकानामसंभेदाय (बृ.उ. ४ । ४ । २२) ।

द्यौः सचन्द्रार्कनक्षत्रा खं दिशो भूर्महोदधिः ।
वासुदेवस्य वीर्येण विधृतानि महात्मनः ॥

इत्यादिषु प्रसिद्धमेतत् ॥ ४॥

The word *anejat* means static, for it is the antonym of *ejat* where *ejr* means vibrate. The word *ekam* means the primary. This would in turn mean the one who has none equal or superior to him. Even those who achieve an extreme similarity with God on attaining *moksha* , would still be dependent on him.

God is *manaso javeeyah* – faster than thought. There is no contradiction in stating God as static and also faster than the fastest. Being present everywhere, he is available at everyplace of which the mind can have a thought. Deities *Brahma, Rudra* etc though have had God with them since long, they have not known him. Though they had God with them on account of him being omnipresent, they had, with their limited knowledge getting further shrunk by their *karma* , not known him till the time they got *upadesha* from their respective Guru. So says *Chaandogya* upanishat "People would not know the treasure hidden underneath while they walk on the ground. Similarly, people do not know God even as they enter him every day (while in sleep). Other upanishats like *Brihadaaranyaka* also describe God as dwelling in earth, dwelling in jeevas, in every object. Hence there is no contradiction in saying that God stays put firm but also is faster than the fastest.

The deity *maatarishvaa* , *vaayu* supports water while he is supported by God. Water here symbolically represents the entire universe including the oceans, stars, planets etc. *Vaayu* does so on account of the strength provided by God. *Brihadaranyaka* upanishat calls God as the supporter of the entire universe who holds it in one piece. This aspect is also popularly stated in other scripts as "the heaven, moon, sun, stars, sky, the cardinal directions, earth and the oceans are all held in place by the power of *Vaasudeva* .

Madhwaachaarya :

अनेजन्निर्भयत्वात्तदेकं प्राधान्यतस्तथा ।
सम्यग्ज्ञातुमशक्यत्वादगम्यं तत्सुरैरपि ।
स्वयं तु सर्वानगमत्पूर्वमेव स्वभावतः ।
अचिन्त्यशक्तितश्चैव सर्वगत्वाच्च तत्परम्।
द्रवतोऽत्येति संतिष्ठत्तस्मिन्कर्माण्यधान्मरुत् ।

मारुत्येव यतश्चेष्टा सर्वा तां हरयेऽर्पयेदि ॥

ति ब्रह्माण्डे ।

ऋष ज्ञाने ॥ ४॥

He (God) does not shake (unwavering) because he is fearless. He is referred to as “One” because he is the main person. It is impossible to know him fully and hence is referred to as unreachable even by deities. He has naturally reached everything before anybody could do so. He could do so by virtue of his unimaginable capabilities and because he is omnipresent. Standing still, he overtakes all those who are running. The deity *vaayu* offers him the *karma*, the deeds of everyone. Since it is *vaayu* who enables the performance of all tasks, he dedicates all the tasks to God. - *Brahmanda puraana.*

The term “ *Rsh* ” in the word *poorvamarshat* means knowledge.

The term *anejat* (immobile) should be understood to mean fearlessness and not inertia or inactivity. The word *poorvamarshat* means omniscience. He knows everything naturally, by virtue of his nature. He does not have to learn or put in efforts to know anything.

तदेजति

तदेजति तन्नैजति तद्दूरे तद्वन्तिके ।

तदन्तरस्य सर्वस्य तदु सर्वस्यास्य बाह्यतः ॥ ५॥

tadejati tannejati taddoore tadvantike |

tadantarasya sarvasya tadu sarvasya baahyatah |5|

Sankaraachaarya : न मन्त्राणां जामितास्तीति पूर्वमन्त्रोक्तमप्यर्थं पुनराह -

There is no restriction on repetitions for Veda. The meaning of what is expressed in the previous mantra is repeated here also.

तत् आत्मतत्त्वं यत्प्रकृतम् एजति चलति तदेव च नैजति स्वतो नैव चलति, स्वतः अचलमेव सत् चलतीवेत्यर्थः । किञ्च, तद्दूरे वर्षकोटिशतैरप्यविदुषामप्राप्यत्वाद्दूर इव । तदु अन्तिके समीपे अत्यन्तमेव विदुषाम् , आत्मत्वात् न केवलं दूरे, अन्तिके च। तत् अन्तः अभ्यन्तरे अस्य सर्वस्य, "य आत्मा सर्वान्तरः" इति श्रुतेः, अस्य सर्वस्य जगतो नामरूपक्रियात्मकस्य । तत् उ सर्वस्य अस्य बाह्यतः , व्यापित्वादाकाशवन्निरतिशयसूक्ष्मत्वादन्तः ; "प्रज्ञानघन एव" (बृ. उ. ४ । ५ । १३) इति शासनान्निरन्तरं च ॥

The hitherto discussed *aatmatatva* , God moves and he does not move. He does not move by himself and remaining immobile, he looks like he is moving. He is there even at a distance of a hundred million light years. He cannot be understood even by the wisest. Hence he is considered as remaining far away. He is very near to the learned. He is not just far and near, he is there in everyone. *Sruti* (*veda*) says *aatma* (God) is within everyone. He is beyond anything that can be identified by a name, shape or action in this world and spread like space. He is even within the minutest of the minute objects. He is referred to as *prajnaanaghana* . Hence there are no gaps within him. He is continuous in spite of being within the minutest and farther than the farthest.

Raamaanujeeya : एवमुपधिष्टविचित्रशक्तित्वमादरेण मुखान्तरेण पुनरनुशास्ति - भूयोभूयः प्रवचनं श्रवणं च कर्तव्यमिति पुनरनुशासनाभिप्रायः । तथा च श्रूयते-

After noting the extraordinary power of God, upanishat speaks out further on the matter, to lay emphasis on it – The glory of God should be repeatedly explained and repeatedly heard. *Mundaka Upanishat* says -

येनाक्षरं पुरुषं वेद सत्यं प्रोवाच तां तत्त्वतो ब्रह्मविद्याम् (मु.उ.१२।१३) इति । तत्त्वतः । अज्ञानसंशयविपर्ययनिरासो यथा भवति तथा प्रोवाच प्रकर्षण ब्रूयात्पुनः पुनरुपदिशेदित्यर्थः।

The factual glory of God, with no room for doubt or an improper understanding, be told again and again.

तदेजति तत्सर्वव्याप्तं ब्रह्मैजति कम्पत इव जवीय इवेति यावत् । तदु तदेव नैजति वस्तुतो न कम्पते । तद्दूरे च तदेवान्तिके च वर्तते । आसुरदैवप्रकृतिकपुरुषभेदापेक्षया विभोरेव दूरान्तिकवर्तित्व-व्यपदेशः । तथाऽऽह भगवाञ्शौनकः-

पराङ्मुखा ये गोविन्दे विषयासक्तचेतसः ।
तेषां तत्परमं ब्रह्म दूराद्दूरतरे स्थितम् ॥
तन्मयत्वेन गोविन्दे ये नरा न्यस्तचेतसः ॥
विषयत्यागिनस्तेषां विज्ञेयं च तदन्तिके ॥ इति ।

Brahma (God), which is omnipresent appears to be moving fast while the fact is, it stays firm. It is available at the far off place as well as in proximity. Since it is omnipresent, the far and near expressions are with reference to the *jeevas* who are of the nature of *aasura* (demon) and *daiva* (deities). *Shounaka muni* says, *Govinda* is farther than than the far for those who have turned their backs towards him and are thus engaged in material pleasures. He is very near to those who have fixed their minds in him and have detached themselves from the material pleasures.

अपरमप्येकं वैचित्र्यमित्याह तत्सर्वव्याप्तं परं ब्रह्मास्य सर्वस्य प्रमाणावगतस्य वस्तुनोऽप्यन्तर्भवति तदेव पुनस्तदानीमेव सर्वस्य बहिरपि भवतीत्यर्थः । तदितरेषां गृहान्तवर्तिनां तदानीं बहिष्ठत्वं न

संभवति बहिर्वसतां च नान्तर्वर्तित्वमिति ब्रह्मणि वैचित्र्यमिति भावः । यद्यप्यणुषु नान्तर्वतिता संभवति तथा प्रतिघातादविभक्तदेशतया वर्तित्वमात्रेणान्तर्वतित्वोक्तिः । एवं बहिर्व्याप्तिरप्यविभुद्रव् यापेक्षयैव । न तु विभुद्रव्यापेक्षयाऽपीति दृष्टव्यम् । तदिदं वैचित्र्यं तैत्तिरीयेऽप्युक्तम्-अन्तर्बहिश्च तत्सर्वं व्याय नारायणः स्थित इति ॥५॥

Upanishat explains another extraordinary quality of God – The omnipresent God stays within every known object. While being so, at the same time, he is outside of every such object. This is peculiar only to him. For, a person cannot be inside a house and also at the same time outside of it.

The expression that God is within everything is with an exception of items of miniature anu size. For, they are considered to be indivisible. Similarly, he is outside everything except those that are considered omnipresent themselves.

This extraordinary quality is also explained in *Taittareeya upanishat* – *Naaraayana* stays fully spread within and outside of every object.

Madhwaachaarya : तदेजति तत एव एजत्यन्यत् । तत्स्वयं नैजति ।

ततो बिभेति सर्वोऽपि न बिभेति हरिः स्वयम् ।
सर्वगत्वात्स दरे च बाह्येऽतश्च समीपगः ॥

इति तत्त्वसंहितायाम् ॥५॥

God is not scared. He scares others. *Tatvasamhita* says as under:

Everything is scared of him but he (*Hari*) has no fear. Since he is omnipresent, he is at the farthest places and also very near. He is within and outside of everything.

यस्तु सर्वाणि

यस्तु सर्वाणि भूतानि आत्मन्येवानुपश्यति ।

सर्वभूतेषु चात्मानं ततो न विजुगुप्सते ॥ ६ ॥

yastu sarvaaNi bhootanyatmnyevaanupaSyati

sarvabhooteShu chaatmaanamtato na vijugupsate |6|

Sankaraachaarya : यस्तु परिव्राट् मुमुक्षुः सर्वाणि भूतानि अव्यक्तादीनि स्थावरान्तानि आत्मन्येव अनुपश्यति, आत्मव्यतिरिक्तानि न पश्यतीत्यर्थः । सर्वभूतेषु तेष्वेव च आत्मानं तेषामपि भूतानां स्वमात्मानमात्मत्वेन - यथास्य देहस्य कार्यकरणसङ्घातस्यात्मा अहं सर्वप्रत्ययसाक्षिभूतश्चेतयिता केवलो निर्गुणोऽनेनैव स्वरूपेणाव्यक्तादीनां स्थावरान्तानामहमेवात्मेति सर्वभूतेषु चात्मानं निर्विशेषं यस्त्वनुपश्यति, सः ततः तस्मादेव दर्शनात् न विजुगुप्सते विजुगुप्सां घृणां न करोति ।

The *sanyaasi* (One who has renounced the world) who is desirous of salvation finds everything, right from *avyakta* (the minutest imperceivable form of matter) to the huge immovable objects, as present in God. In other words, he does not find them as any different from God. Not only that, he also finds God in all those objects.

The body I have is nothing but a collection of causes and effects. I am responsible for the activities of this body while I derive the knowledge of other objects through it. Similarly, the same me, who is no different than God in the natural unqualified form, stay in this universe as its soul and is responsible for the activity of everything in this universe. Whoever realizes this fact will, on account of such realization, ceases to discriminate.

प्राप्तस्यैवानुवादोऽयम् । सर्वा हि घृणा आत्मनोऽन्यद्दुष्टं पश्यतो भवति; आत्मान-मेवात्यन्तविशुद्धं निरन्तरं पश्यतो न घृणानिमित्त-मर्थान्तरमस्तीति प्राप्तमेव - ततो न विजुगुप्सत इति ॥

Thus it deduces as under. All the hatred is due to finding faults with another. When one realizes the entire is himself in pure form with no difference, there is no room for anything that can cause hatred. Once the aforesaid universality is realized, there is no reason for such discrimination.

Raamaanujeeya : एवं सर्वस्य ब्रह्मात्मकत्वमुक्तम् । अथ सर्वं जगद्ब्रह्मात्मकमित्यनुसंदधानस्यैहिकं प्रयोजनमाह -

Having told that everything in the universe is full of God, upanishat now speaks of the material benefit a person would derive out of such an understanding.

यः परमात्मज्ञानाधिकृतः सर्वाणि भूतानि ब्रह्मादिस्तम्बपर्यन्तान्या-त्मन्येव परमात्मन्येवानुस्यूतानि पश्यति ध्यायतीत्यर्थः। पृथिव्यादि-ध्रियमाणमपि तन्मुखेन परमात्मन्येव स्थितमित्येवकाराभिप्रायः ।तुशब्देनास्याधिकारिणो माहात्म्यविशेषो द्योत्यते । किंच सर्वभूतेषु चाऽऽत्मानं परमात्मानं यः पश्यतीति । इदं व्याप्तिमात्रपरम् । परमपुरुषस्यानन्याधारत्वादिति भावः । यच्छब्दस्य स इति प्रतिनिर्देशोऽध्याहार्यः । स उक्तविधज्ञानी । ततस्तेषु सप्तम्यर्थे तसिः । ब्रह्मात्मकतया दृष्टेषु सर्वेषु भूतेष्वित्यर्थः । न विजुगुप्सते कुतश्चिदपि न बीभत्सते । स्वात्मविभूतिन्यायेन क्वचिदपि निन्दा न करोतीति भावः ॥६॥

One who is qualified for securing knowledge of God, sees (understands) that everything in this world, right from *Brahma* (*Chaturmukha*) up to a blade of grass (and even the miniature objects), is embedded in God and meditates as such. Those seen as supported by the earth etc are also supported by God through the earth etc. The letter ' *tu* ' in the mantra indicates the special status of the one who is eligible to secure knowledge of God. Such a person would see God as occupying everything. This occupancy speaks only of the omnipresence but not dependence on such other objects for sustenance. A *jnaani* who has thus understood the presence of God in and out of everything would not shy away. He would consider everything as the glory of God and hence would never criticize anything.

Madhwaachaarya :

सर्वगं परमात्मानं सर्वं च परमात्मनि।
यः पशयेत्स भयाभावान्नात्मानं गोप्तुमिच्छति ॥

इति सौकरायणश्रुतिः ॥६॥

Whoever finds every thing in God and God in everything; he has no fear and hence does not hide himself. This is quoted from the soukaraayana text of vedas.

In the previous mantra, the omnipresence of God was explained. This one depicts the fruits of its understanding

यस्मिन्सर्वाणि

यस्मिन्सर्वाणि भूतानि आत्मैवाभूद्विजानतः ।

तत्र को मोहः कः शोक एकत्वमनुपश्यतः ॥ ७ ॥

yasmin sarvaaNi bhootan-yatmaiva-abhood-vijaanatah|

tatra ko mohah kaSSoka ekatvam-anupaSyatah |7|

Sankaraachaarya : इममेवार्थमन्योऽपि मन्त्र आह -

यस्मिन्सर्वाणि भूतानि यस्मिन् काले यथोक्तात्मनि वा, तान्येव भूतानि सर्वाणि परमार्थात्मदर्शनात् आत्मैवाभूत् आत्मैव संवृत्तः परमार्थवस्तु विजानतः, तत्र तस्मिन्काले तत्रात्मनि वा, को मोहः कः शोकः । शोकश्च मोहश्च कामकर्मबीजमजानतो भवति, न त्वात्मैकत्वं विशुद्धं गगनोपमं पश्यतः ।

The intent of the previous mantra is repeated through another mantra-

At the time when one realizes that everything is in God, on account of such realization, everything becomes God. At the time of such realization of God, he would not have any misapprehension and no suffering. Sufferings and misapprehension arise out of desire-laced acts. They do not affect the wise, who have realized the unity of God like the sky with every being.

को मोहः कः शोक इति शोकमोहयोरविद्याकार्ययोराक्षेपेणासम्भव-प्रकाशनात् सकारणस्य संसारस्यात्यन्तमेवोच्छेदः प्रदर्शितो भवति ॥

Upanishat says "where is misapprehension, where is sorrow" to strongly negate their existence in a person who has had the aforesaid realization. Misapprehension and sorrow are the effects of improper knowledge. Once this cause is removed, it removes its outcome, the cycle of births and deaths.

Raamaanujeeya : एवं वैयधिकरण्येनोक्तं सर्वस्य ब्रह्मात्मकत्वं सामानाधिकरण्येनापि द्रढयंस्तदनुध्यानस्य सद्यः शोकनिवर्तकत्वमाह -

In the previous mantra, *jeeva* and God are considered as different while saying that everything is God. This mantra emphasizes the same fact of God being everything by considering God and others as one and the same. It also says that such a knowledge would immediately remove the sorrows.

यस्मिन्प्रणिधानसमये विजानत ईशावास्यमित्यारभ्य ततो न विजुगुप्सत इत्यन्तेनोपदिष्टं स्वतन्त्रं परतन्त्रं वस्तुभेदं यथोपदेशं विविच्य जानत इत्यर्थः । नन्वेवमत्यन्तभेदाभ्युपगमे सर्वाणि भूतान्यात्मेवाभूदिति सामानाधिकरण्यं भज्यतेत्याशङ्कावारणाय यस्य पृथिवी शरीरम् । (बृ. उ.३।२।१३) यस्य शरीरम् (बृ. उ. ३।७।३) इत्यादिघटक.श्रुतिसिद्धसंबन्धविशेषमाह - एकत्वमनुपश्यत इति । आकृतिव्यक्त्योरिव गुणगुणिनोरिव चात्यन्तभिन्नयोरेव जगद्ब्रह्मणोरेकत्वं विभागानर्हसंबन्धविशेषं पश्यतो विशदमनुध्यायत इत्यर्थः । रामसुग्रीवयोरैक्यं देव्यर्थं समजायत । इत्यादाविवेहाप्येकशब्दस्य संबन्धविशेष एवार्थो विवक्षितुं युक्त इति भावः । एवं च सर्वाणि भूतान्यात्मैवाभूदिति सर्वभूतशरीरकः प्रतीतोऽभूदित्यर्थः ।

While reading the initial *mantras* beginning with *eeshaavaasyam* up to *vijugupsate* , one understands that God and Jeeva, being independent and dependent respectively, are different from each other. This however contradicts the statement " *sarvaani bhootaani aatmaivaabhoot* – all things became God". In order to remove this confusion, we need to consider the statements of *Brihadaaranyaka Upanishat – yasya prithivee shareeram, yasya shareeram* etc to understand the intent of " *ekatvam anupashyatah* " of the current mantra. The word ekatvam which is generally taken to mean unity / oneness, has other meanings as well in its usage. To illustrate, the shape of an object and the object are considered one and the same. Similar is the case with the attributes of an object and the object. They are inherently different. The color of rose is not rose. The shape of an elephant is not the elephant. Similarly God and the universe are different but are considered as one only because of their inseparable relationship.

The expression that Rama and Sugreeva became one for the purpose of securing Seeta is another example where the expression of oneness is intended to present a relationship.

तत्राऽऽदौ प्रणिधानसमये को मोहः । स्वतन्त्रादिभ्रमादिलक्षणो मोहो न संभवति । कः शोकः परमात्मविभूतितयाऽवगते सर्वस्मिन्निर्ममत्व-सिद्धौ पुत्रादिमरणराज्यादिहरणादावपि न कश्चिच्छोकः स्यादित्यर्थः । यथाऽऽह -

यस्य मे चास्ति सर्वत्र यस्य मे नास्ति किंचन ।
मिथिलायां प्रदीप्तायां न मे किंचन दह्यते ॥ इति ।

In the beginning, while the seeker prays, he had no illusion of being independent. After learning that everything is just the magnificence of God and that it belongs to him, the seeker now discards the sense of belonging, "mine" from everything and hence would remain undaunted even with the great miseries like son's death or loss of kingdom. So goes a saying:

When a person feels that he has nothing, while having everything, how would it matter for him if the city of Mithila burns?

अत्र केचित्सर्वाणि भूतान्यात्मैवाभूदिति बाधायां सामानाधिकरण्यम् । तथा च सर्वाणि भूतान्यात्मव्यतिरिक्तानि न सन्तीत्यर्थः । यथा चोरः स्थाणुरिति । स्थाणुरेवायं न चोर इत्यर्थः । तथेहापीत्याहुः। अन्ये तु नरपतिरेव सर्वे लोका इतिवदौपचारिकमिदं सामानाधिकरण्यम् । नरपत्यधीनाः सर्वे जना इति हि तन्निर्वाहस्तदिहापि परमात्माधीनानि सर्वाणि भूतानीति भाव इति वर्णयन्ति । अपरे तु घटशरावादयः सर्वे मृत्पिण्डा एवेतिवज्जगद्ब्रह्मणोरेकद्रव्यत्वं परिकल्प्यैवेदं सामानाधि-करण्यं निर्वाह्यमित्याचक्षते । सिद्धान्तस्तु देवोऽहं मनुष्योऽहमित्यादि-वच्छरीरात्मभावसंबन्धेनैव जगब्रह्मणोः सामानाधिकरण्यनिर्वाहे संभवति सति बाधोपचारस्वरूपैक्यपक्षा वैदिकैर्बहिष्कार्याः ॥७॥

Since it is illogical to say that everything became one with God, some say that it only means that anything other than God did not exist. It is something like when a person says "the *sthaanu* (branch-less trunk of a tree) was the thief". It only means that the *sthaanu* was mistaken to be thief while there was no thief there. Others say that the oneness is intended to highlight the power and control God wields over the universe, as when it is said that everything here is the King himself. Some others speak of oneness in the context of common material as when some one says all these earthen articles of pot, stove, hot pan etc are nothing but clay.

The truth is, the oneness stated here is similar to the usage "I am a diety" "I am human" etc where the body is considered as one with the dwelling jeeva in view of the deep relationship between one another. The oneness of God with the universe is similar to such usage. This being so, the thought that God himself is the universe should be thrown out by the believers in Veda.

Madhwaachaarya : यस्मिन्परमात्मनि सर्वभूतानि स परमात्मैव तत्र सर्वभूतेष्वभूत् । एवं सर्वभूतेष्वेकत्वेन परमात्मानं विजानत: को मोहः ।

God, in whom everything is present, is himself present in everything. Whoever knows him this way that he is one in everything, has no misapprehensions left in him.

Pippalaada Sruti (Vedic text) says as under:

यस्मिन्सर्वाणि भूतानि स आत्मा सर्वभूतग: ।
एवं सर्वत्र यो विष्णुं पश्येत्तस्य विजानतः ।
को मोहः कोऽथवा शोकः स विष्णुं पर्यगाद्यत: ॥

इति पिप्पलादशाखायाम् ॥

In whom everything is located, that God is within everything. Whoever understands *ViShnu* (another name of God) to be so, he has no misapprehensions or sorrows since he has got (realized) God.

पूर्वेक्तानुवादेन शोकमोहाभावोऽपि विजानतश्चात्रोच्यते। अभ्यासश्च सर्वगतत्वस्य तात्पर्यद्योतनार्थः ॥७॥

While the previous mantra has explained the fearlessness as the fruit of knowing the omnipresence of God, this one extends it further to the removal of misapprehensions and sorrow as results of such realization. The repetitive expression of omnipresence denotes greater emphasis.

स पर्यगाच्छुक्रम्

स पर्यगाच्छुक्रमकायमव्रणमस्नाविरं शुद्धमपापविद्धम् ।

कविर्मनीषी परिभूः स्वयम्भूर्याथातथ्यतोऽर्थान् व्यदधाच्छाश्वतीभ्यः समाभ्यः ॥ ८ ॥

sa paryagaac-chukram akaayam-avraNam

asnaaviram Suddham-apaapaviddham |

kavirmaneeshee paribhoo-svayambhoo

yaathaa-tathyato-rthaan vyadadhaac-

chaaSvateebhyas-samaabhyah |8|

Sankaraachaarya : योऽयमतीतैर्मन्त्रैरुक्त आत्मा, स स्वेन रूपेण किंलक्षण इत्याह अयं मन्त्रः -

This mantra describes the characteristics of God, referred to in the previous *mantra* , in his original form.

स पर्यगात् , सः यथोक्त आत्मा पर्यगात् परि समन्तात् अगात् गतवान् , आकाशवद्व्यापीत्यर्थः । शुक्रं शुभ्रं ज्योतिष्मत् दीप्तिमानित्यर्थः । अकायम् अशरीरं लिङ्गशरीरवर्जित इत्यर्थः । अव्रणम् अक्षतम् । अस्नाविरम् स्नावाः सिरा यस्मिन्न विद्यन्त इत्यस्नाविरम् । अव्रणमस्नाविरमित्येताभ्यां स्थूलशरीरप्रतिषेधः । शुद्धं निर्मलम-विद्यामलरहितमिति कारणशरीरप्रतिषेधः । अपापविद्धं धर्माधर्मा-दिपापवर्जितम् । शुक्रमित्यादीनि वचांसि पुंलिङ्गत्वेन परिणेयानि, स पर्यगात् इत्युपक्रम्य कविर्मनीषी इत्यादिना पुंलिङ्गत्वेनोपसंहारात् ।

Aforesaid God is encompassing everything and is omnipresent like space. He is *shukram* - pure and radiant. He is *akaayam* - devoid of a body. He does not have even the basic subtle covering called *linga Sareera* . He is *avranam* - free from injury / loss. *Asnaaviram* - He does not have ligament / vascular tissues etc. These references of injury and ligaments convey that God does not have a material body. He is *shuddham* - pure – is devoid of the impurity of wrongful knowledge, a negation of a created body. *Apaapaviddham* - He is devoid of the fruits of righteous and sinful acts.

The above words *Sukram, akaayam, avraNam, asnaaviram, apaapaviddham* are in neutral gender. They have to be interpreted as referring to masculine gender to match the further references like *kavi* etc.

कविः क्रान्तदर्शी सर्वदृक् , "नान्योऽतोऽस्ति द्रष्टा" (बृ. उ. ३ । ७ । २३) इत्यादिश्रुतेः । मनीषी मनस ईषिता, सर्वज्ञ ईश्वर इत्यर्थः । परिभूः सर्वेषां परि उपरि भवतीति परिभूः । स्वयम्भूः स्वयमेव भवतीति, येषामुपरि भवति यश्चोपरि भवति स सर्वः स्वयमेव भवतीति स्वयम्भूः ।

He is *kavi* meaning, he who has seen beyond the present. He sees everything past present and future. Vedas say that there is no one who has seen anything beyond what God has seen. He is *maneeshee* , the lord of mind – omniscient. He is *paribhoo* - stays above everything. He manifests on his own. That which stays above and that is below, it is all him alone. Hence he is called *swayambhoo* .

स नित्यमुक्त ईश्वरः याथातथ्यतः सर्वज्ञत्वात् यथातथाभावो याथातथ्यं तस्मात् यथाभूतकर्मफलसाधनतः अर्थान् कर्तव्यपदार्थान् व्यदधात् विहितवान् , यथानुरूपं व्यभजदित्यर्थः । शाश्वतीभ्यः नित्याभ्यः समाभ्यः संवत्सराख्येभ्यः प्रजापतिभ्य इत्यर्थः ॥

That eternally liberated God who is omniscient allocates the tasks to all beings right from *Prajaapati* (the supreme amongst deities, who is in-charge of creation) based on the fruits they deserve. He does this at all times eternally.

अत्राद्येन मन्त्रेण सर्वैषणापरित्यागेन ज्ञाननिष्ठोक्ता प्रथमो वेदार्थः "ईशावास्यमिदं सर्वम् मा गृधः कस्य स्विद्धनम्" (ई. उ. १) इति अज्ञानां जिजीविषूणां ज्ञाननिष्ठासम्भवे "कुर्वन्नेवेह कर्माणि जिजीविषेत्" (ई. उ. २) इति कर्मनिष्ठोक्ता द्वितीयो वेदार्थः । अनयोश्च निष्ठयोर्विभागो मन्त्रद्वयप्रदर् शितयोर्बृहदारण्यकेऽपि दर्शितः - "सोऽकामयत जाया मे स्यात्" (बृ. उ. १ । ४ । १७) इत्यादिना अज्ञस्य कामिनः कर्माणीति । "मन एवास्यात्मा वाग्जाया" (बृ. उ. १ । ४ । १७), (बृ. उ. १ । ५ ।

२) इत्यादिवचनात् अज्ञत्वं कामित्वं च कर्मनिष्ठस्य निश्चितमवगम्यते । तथा च तत्फलं सप्तान्नसर्गस्तेष्वात्म-भावेनात्मस्वरूपावस्थानम् ।

Through the first mantra " *eesaavasyamidam... kasyaswiddhanam* ", this Upanishat speaks of the progress through renunciation of desires of wealth, women and ones own off springs. This is for those who adopt the path of knowledge. As for others who cannot go in the path of knowledge but desire to live through, it preaches the performance of duties in the second mantra " *kurvanneveha... karmaaNi* ". Even *BrihadaaraNyaka Upanishat* tells the same classification of paths through "He desired to have a wife" etc. It prescribes performance of karma, the tasks to those ignorant who have worldly desires. The sayings like "Mind is himself and the voice is his wife" specify that ignorance and desire are definitely the qualities of those in the path of karma. Such activities result in fetching seven different kinds of food. These are: 1. Cereals etc for humans, 2. *huta* and 3. *prahuta* (both of them refer to offerings in sacrificial fire – they are food for deities). 4. Mind 5. Speech and 6. Breath (These three are food for the soul) and 7. Milk for animals.

जायाद्येषणात्रयसंन्यासेन चात्मविदां कर्मनिष्ठाप्रातिकूल्येन आत्मस्वरूपनिष्ठैव दर्शिता - "किं प्रजया करिष्यामो येषां नोऽयमात्मायं लोकः" (बृ. उ. ४ । ४ । २२) इत्यादिना । ये तु ज्ञाननिष्ठाः संन्यासिनस्तेभ्यः "असुर्या नाम ते" (ई. उ. ३) इत्यादिना अविद्वन्निन्दाद्वारेणात्मनो याथात्म्यम् "स पर्यगात्" (ई. उ. ८) इत्येतदन्तैर्मन्त्रैरुपदिष्टम् । ते ह्यत्राधिकृता न कामिन इति । तथा च श्वेताश्वतराणां मन्त्रोपनिषदि - "अत्याश्रमिभ्यः परमं पवित्रं प्रोवाच सम्यगृषिसङ्घजुष्टम्" (श्वे. उ. ६ । २१) इत्यादि विभज्योक्तम् । ये तु कामिनः कर्मनिष्ठाः कर्म कुर्वन्त एव जिजीविषवः, तेभ्य इदमुच्यते

Those who renounce the three desires of Wife, Wealth and Children are in the path of knowledge unlike those who engage themselves in the performance of duties. They say "what will I do with children when my world is God". It is for these persons that the Upanishat cautions against adopting wrong knowledge that leads to the dark worlds and preaches the true nature of God with the subsequent mantras till the last one " *sa paryagaat* ...". Only those who have renounced desires are eligible for the path of knowledge. So says *SwetaSwatara Upanishat* :

"(He) spoke of the highly sacred path followed by those in the supreme *aashrama* (renounced living) and adopted by the sages". These and other texts demarcate the path of *karma* from that of *jnaana* , knowledge. The following mantras are for those who are in the path of *karma* and like to live with it.

Raamaanujeeya : पुनरप्येनमीशेशितव्यवेदिनं वेदितव्येश्वरस्व-हेयशोधनेन विशिष्टज्ञानयोगादिकमप्युपदिशति -

The upanishat again preaches *jnaana yoga* that is signified by the distinction between God and others through rejection of oneness with God, by the one who has by now understood God as the lord and others as his subjects.

यः सर्वभूतान्तरात्मब्रह्मदर्शी स पर्यगात्प्राप्नुयादित्यर्थः । "ब्रह्मविदाप्नोति परम्" । (तै.उ.२।१।१) इति न्यायात् । यद्वा समाधिलब्धेनानुभवेन प्राप्नुयादिति सिद्धानुवादः । "अत्र ब्रह्म समश्नुते" । (बृ. उ. ४।४।७) इतिवत् । शुक्रमवदातं स्वप्रकाशमित्यर्थः । अकायम् । सर्वशरीरकमपि कर्मकृतहेयशरीररहितमित्यर्थः। न तस्य प्राकृता मूर्तिः मांसमेदोस्थिसंभवा। इतिहेयशरीरस्यैवान्यत्र प्रतिषेधदर्शनात् । न तु दिव्यमङ्गलविग्रहरहितमित्यर्थः। "यत्ते रूपं कल्याणतमं तत् पश्यामि ।" (ई.उ.१६) "य एषोऽन्तराऽऽदित्ये हिरण्मयः पुरुषो दृश्यते ॥ (मै.६।१) "आदित्यवर्णं तमसः परस्तात् (श्वे.उ. ३।८) इत्याद्युपनिषत्प्रसिद्ध स्वाप्राकृतविग्रहस्य निषेधायोगादिति भावः । अव्रणम् । कर्मजन्यशरीराभावादेवाक्षतम् । अस्नाविरं च । स्नावाः शिरा यस्मिन्विद्यन्ते तत्स्नाविरम् । स्नाविरं न भवतीत्यस्नाविरम् । शुद्धम् । अनाघ्राताज्ञानादिदोषगन्धम् । अशनपानादिषडूर्मिरहितं च । अपापविद्धम् । अज्ञानादेः कार्यकारण-भूतैः पुण्यपापरूपकर्मभिरलीढमित्यर्थः । "न शोको न सुकृतं न दुष्कृतम्"। (छा.उ. ८।४।१) इत्यारभ्य "सर्वे पाप्मानोऽतो निवर्तन्ते" इति पापशब्देनोपसंहारदर्शनात् । स्वर्गादिहेतुभूतविशेषस्यापीह पापशब्देन संग्रहणमिति भावः ।

एवमहेयहेयप्रत्यनीकं परमात्मानं स विद्वान्पर्यगादिति पूर्वेण संबन्धः।

He who sees God everywhere gets God. So says *Taittareeya Upanishat* – He who knows *Brahma* would get him. It also means that he would have got God during his deep meditation called as *samaadhi* . This interpretation is on the lines of *Brihadaaranyaka Upanishat* statement "Here he gets *Brahma* ".

God is described here as *shukram* – white – luminous, *akaayam* – Does not have a body as a consequence of his *karma* , his past deeds, though everything in the universe is his body. It is only an inferior body that is said to be non existing in him. Scripts say "he does not have a material body made of flesh and blood". However, they do not negate every kind of body. He does have a divine flawless body and not a material one. So say the scripts – I see his magnificent body, He is the golden one who is seen inside the Sun, He has the colour of Sun etc. He is *avranam* – does not have even a scratch on his body, for the body is not got as a result of *karma* . *Asnaaviram* – *snaava* means connectors (blood vessels, tendons, nerves etc). God does not have a body made of components having channels – blood vessels, nerves, tendons etc. *Suddham* – He does not even smell any kind of defects like *ajnaana* (ignorance or incorrect knowledge). He is free from the six pains of eating and drinking etc. *Apaapaviddham* – untainted by the sins and virtues caused by karma arising out of *ajnaana* . *Chandogya Upanishat* explains this in detail – He has no pain, no virtue no sin. Every sin runs away from him. Even the virtues that cause temporary heavens are also classified as equivalent to sin here.

A *jnaani* will obtain God, who is different from all the worldly aspects whether they are desirables or avoidances.

एवंरूपः परमात्मा प्राप्यः प्रापक उपास्यश्च यस्य तं ब्रह्मविदं विशिनष्टि कविः। व्यासादिवद्ब्रह्मस्व रूपरूपदिव्यगुणादिप्रकाशकप्रबन्ध-विशेषाणां निर्मातेत्यर्थः । अथवा क्रान्तदर्शी । कर्मयोगस्तु

कुर्वन्नेवेह कर्माणीति मन्त्रेण पुरस्तादेवोक्तः । अथ ज्ञानयोगसाध्यप्रत्यगात्म-साक्षात्कारहेतुभूतं जीवात्मयोगमाह - मनीषी मनस ईशित्री बुद्धिर्मनीषा, तद्वान्मनीषी भगवत्स्वरूपगुणस्मृत्यभ्यासेन तदितर-विषयवैराग्येण च प्रतिष्ठितप्रज्ञ इत्यर्थः । परिभूः कामक्रोधादीन्परि-भवतीति परिभूः । अनेन विरोधिनिवृत्तिरूपयोगाङ्गसेवनमुक्तम् । योगाभ्यासफलमाह - स्वयंभूः । अन्यनिरपेक्षसत्ताकः सुखरूपतया स्वात्मदर्शीति यावत् । याथातथ्यतः । यथावद्विविच्य । अर्थान् प्रष्टव्यार्थान् । तस्य वाचकः प्रणवस्तज्जपस्तदर्थभावनमितिसूत्रोक्तान् व्यधाद्धृदयेन धृतवानित्यर्थः । सर्वान्तरायप्रशमनार्थमिति भावः ।

Kavi – A person for whom the aforesaid God is the destiny, the means and the subject of *upaasana* (listening, critical examination and meditation). The word also means the one who is like *Vedavyaasa* , author of books that publicizes the extraordinary heavenly qualities of God. Another meaning is, the one who sees beyond the visible. *Karmayoga* has been explained earlier through the *mantra kurvanneva* etc. Now, upanishat presents the *jeevaatma yoga,* as a means to achieve *jnaanayoga* that leads to *saakshaatkaara* , the physical perception of God. *Maneeshi* – the lord of mind, *buddhi* – the intellect is *maneesha* . One who possesses it is *maneeshi* . He is the one who has repeatedly remembered the inherent qualities of God and thereby achieved a stable intellect by discarding the desire for material objects. *Paribhoo* – one who has surpassed the defects of *kaama* and *krodha* (desire and anger). This explains the component of *yoga* that is in the form of removal of obstacles. The result of yoga is *Svayambhoo* – One who stays independent of any support from others. In other words, one who sees himself as an embodiment of pleasure. *Yaathaatathyatah arthaan* – One who distinctly sees the exact meaning of texts. *Sootra* says " *tasya vaacahakah pranavah tajjapah tadarthabhaavanam* " - The word Om speaks of Him. Knowing him is his *japa. Vyadadhaat* carries in his heart – for eliminating all obstacles.

यद्वा शुक्रमित्यादि द्वितीयान्तपदजातं परिशुद्धजीवपरम् । तमपि स परमात्मा पर्यगात्परितो व्याप्य स्थित इति प्रथमान्तपदजातं परमात्मपरं योजनीयम् । तथाहि कविः सर्वदर्शी श्रीपञ्चरात्रादिप्रणेतेति वा । मनीषी मनःप्रभृतीनां जीवकरणानां नियन्ता । परितो भवतीति परिभूः सर्वव्यापी स्वयमेव संभवतीति स्वयंभूः । बहुधा विजायत इतिश्रुत्युक्तप्रसिद्धावतारशाली । अत्र कविरित्यादिना कल्याणगुणविधानात् । छान्दोग्ये - "एष आत्माऽपहतपाप्मा विजरो विमृत्युर्विशोको विजिघत्सोऽपिपासः । (छा.उ. ८.१५) इति हेयगुणान्प्रतिषिध्य सत्यकामः सत्यसंकल्प इति कल्याणगुणविधानाच्च निर्गुणं निरञ्जनमित्यादिसामान्यनिषेधस्य हेयगुणविषयत्वं सुगमम् । याथातथ्यत इति । अर्थान्कार्यपदार्थान् शाश्वतीभ्यः समाभ्यो यावद्विलयमवस्थातुं याथातथ्यतो यथावद्विविच्योत्पादितवान्न पुनरेन्द्रजालिकत्वेन बलं प्रकाशितवानिति भावः ॥८॥

An alternate meaning for this mantra is as follows:

The attributes *shukram, akaayam, avranam, asnaaviram, shuddham, apaapaviddham* describe the flawless *jeeva* . The word *paryagaat* means, God has covered even such a jeeva. The words *kavih, maneeshi, paribhoo, swayambhoo* are attributes of God. *Kavi* means who has known everything, who has written the sacred *pancharatraagama* etc. *Maneeshi* , one who is regulating the *manas* and other *indriyas* (senses) of all *jeevas* . He is *paribhoo* since he is present everywhere . He is *swayambhoo* , for he manifests in different forms like Rama, Krishna etc on his own. The word *kavi* also signifies presence of all *kalyaana gunas* – flawless qualities. *Chandogya Upanishat* negates the presence of all negative attributes as "this *aatma* is free from the defects of sin, moderate qualities, death, sorrow, hunger and thirst" and asserts presence of positive qualities as " *satyakaama* and *satyasankalpa* " - his desires are always met and his decisions never fail. Thus, the scripts that say him to be *nirguna* and *niranjana* do so to negate negative attributes only. The expression *yaathaathathyatah vyadadhaat shaashvateebhyah samaabhyah* means that God has created the real universe that stays years and years and years till the ultimate deluge and is not an illusion created out of magic.

Madhwaachaarya : शुक्रं तच्छोकराहित्यादव्रणं नित्यपूर्णतः । पावनत्वात्सदा शुद्धमकायं लिंगवर्जनात् । स्थूलदेहस्य राहित्याद-स्नाविर मुदाहृतम् । एवं भूतोऽपि सार्वज्ञात्कविरित्येव शब्द्यते । ब्रह्मादिसर्वमनसां प्रकृतेर्मनसोऽपि च । ईशितृत्वान्मनीषी स परिभूः सर्वतो वरः । सदाऽनन्याश्रयत्वाच्च स्वयम्भूः परिकीर्तितः । स सत्यं जगदेतादृङ्गित्थमेव प्रवाहतः । अनाद्यनन्तकालेषु प्रवाहैकप्रकारतः । नियमेनैव ससृजे भगवान्पुरुषोत्तमः । सज्ज्ञानानन्दशीर्षोऽसौ सज्ज्ञानानन्दबाहकः । सज्ज्ञानानन्ददेहश्च सज्ज्ञानानन्दपादवान् । एवं भूतो महाविष्णुर्यथार्थं जगदीदृशम् । अनाद्यनन्तकालीनं ससर्जात्मेच्छया प्रभुः इति वाराहे ॥८॥

Varaaha purana says: " *Sukram* means absence of *Soka* , Sorrow. *Avranam* (that which is devoid of any loss) means eternally complete. He is *Suddham* , pure because he is the most sacred. He is *akaaya* , formless because he does not have *linga deha* , the subtlest of the coverings of soul. He is referred to as *asnaavira* , devoid of ligaments and flesh because he does not have any physical body. Even in the absence of any material body, he is omniscient and hence he is called *kavi* , the learned. He is the regulator of all mental activities of all living beings including *prakriti* , the supreme goddess (who is second to only the ultimate God) and *Brahma* the creator of this universe. He is *paribhoo* , superior to everyone. He is *swayambhoo* , meaning ever independent. He does not depend on anybody for anything at any time. He always creates the realistic worlds like the present one continuously, one after the other like water that flows in a river. He is omnipotent and is the supreme most being. (Is it then that he does not have any body? If so how can he be a creator, be wise, be a regulator and so on? We see activities in the world only with those who possess a body to accomplish such tasks. As if to answer this question, *Varaaha purana* explains further). He has a body made of nothing but *saj-jnaana-ananda* - 'truth, knowledge and pleasure' (This word has a vast meaning and only one face of it as it appears when split in the simplest form is given here). His head is made of this substance (*sajjnaanaanda*), so are his hands. His body is of this substance as also his legs. Lord Vishnu characterized by such a body has been creating the realistic worlds like the one we are seeing. He has been creating them since time infinite and will do it eternally. He does all this out of his own will and he is capable of doing it independently".

It is seen in the world that if someone can create any thing, he does so through his body. Thus logically, if we say that God has created the universe he must be having a body. It is also seen in the world that whoever has a body has it growing and degenerating, bringing in pleasures and pains and so on. Thus, God must also be experiencing growth, degeneration, pains etc. If we say he has no form/body, he is not a creator. If we accept that he has a body, it becomes imperative that he has growth, degeneration, pains etc.

The above mantra and the quoted verses from *Varaha puraNa,* step in to resolve this conflict. God does not have any material form / body that causes or facilitates sin and suffering in him. But he is not formless. He has a body and that is not made of matter. Whatever is seen as perpetrator of sin and suffering in the world is the materialistic body and He is beyond matter. He does not create the unrealistic illusory universe like the objects created by a magician. A magician creates or shows us non-existent objects using tricks since he is not capable of creating the realistic things. There is no such constraint for God. He is all capable and independent and hence creates the real objects.

In the previous two mantras, it is explained that the fruits of knowing the omnipresence of God is fearlessness, absence of pain, sorrow and misapprehensions. How does this happen? The Upanishat says, it is due to obtaining/reaching God. Well, it is something like obtaining / reaching an emperor. If we are with an emperor, he takes care of our needs. However, we see the emperor himself as having pains and sufferings and hence is not capable of removing all our pains. Unlike an emperor, God does not have such limitations. It is with this intention that Upanishat further explains his qualities in this mantra.

अन्धं तमः प्रविशन्ति

अन्धं तमः प्रविशन्ति ये अविद्यामुपासते ।

ततो भूय इव ते तमो य उ विद्यायां रताः ॥ ९ ॥

andham tamah praviSanti ye avidyaam upaasate |

tato bhooya iva te tamo ya vu vidyaayaagm rataah |9|

Sankaraachaarya : कथं पुनरेवमवगम्यते, न तु सर्वेषाम् इति?

How then is it known that these *mantras* are only for those in the path of *karma* and not for all?

उच्यते - अकामिनः साध्यसाधनभेदोपमर्देन "यस्मिन्सर्वाणि भूतानि आत्मैवाभूद्विजानतः । तत्र को मोहः कः शोक एकत्वमनुपश्यतः" (ई. उ. ७) इति यत् आत्मैकत्वविज्ञानम् , तन्न केनचित्कर्मणा ज्ञानान्तरेण वा ह्यमूढः समुच्चिचीषति । इह तु समुच्चिचीषया अविद्वदादिनिन्दा क्रियते । तत्र च यस्य येन समुच्चयः सम्भवति न्यायतः शास्त्रतो वा तदिहोच्यते । तद्दैवं वित्तं देवताविषयं ज्ञानं कर्मसम्बन्धित्वेनोपन्यस्तं न परमात्मज्ञानम् , "विद्यया देवलोकः" (बृ. उ. १ । ५ । १६) इति पृथक्फलश्रवणात् ।

The knowledge of unity of soul and God achieved by a *sanyaasi* by practicing the path as told in the *mantra* " *yasmin sarvaaNi* ..", cannot be comprehended by any rational person through *karma* or through any other knowledge. This *mantra* , with an intent to consolidate the position, deplores the unwise. This *mantra* speaks of what can coexist logically and as per scripts. That knowledge which has been referred to as obtainable through *karma* is the knowledge of deities, not of God. Upanishat says "knowledge fetches heaven" making this fact clear.

तयोर्ज्ञानकर्मणोरिहैकैकानुष्ठाननिन्दा समुच्चिचीषया, न निन्दापरैव एकैकस्य, पृथक्फलश्रवणात् - "विद्यया तदारोहन्ति" "विद्यया देवलोकः" (बृ. उ. १ । ५ । १६) "न तत्र दक्षिणा यान्ति" "कर्मणा पितृलोकः" (बृ. उ. १ । ५ । १६) इति । न हि शास्त्रविहितं किञ्चिदकर्तव्यतामियात्

Upanishat deplores the practice of *jnaana* (knowledge) and *karma* (performance) as a combination and not in isolation. For, the scripts describe the benefits of such actions. To illustrate a few - "They ascend through knowledge", "The world of deities is achieved through knowledge", "Those in the southern path (black magic, witchcraft etc) cannot reach there", "The world of *pitr* (deities representing the departed souls) is achieved through the path of performance". Nothing prescribed by scriptures is a prohibited action.

तत्र अन्धं तमः अदर्शनात्मकं तमः प्रविशन्ति । के ? ये अविद्याम् , विद्याया अन्या अविद्या कर्मेत्यर्थः, कर्मणो विद्याविरोधित्वात् , तामविद्यामग्निहोत्रादिलक्षणामेव केवलाम् उपासते तत्पराः सन्तोऽनुतिष्ठन्तीत्यभिप्रायः । ततः तस्मादन्धात्मकात्तमसः भूय इव बहुतरमेव ते तमः प्रविशन्ति । के ? कर्म हित्वा ये उ ये तु विद्यायामेव देवताज्ञाने एव रताः अभिरताः ॥

तत्रावान्तरफलभेदं विद्याकर्मणोः समुच्चयकारणमाह । अन्यथा फलवदफलवतोः संनिहितयोरङ्गाङ्गितया जामितैव स्यादिति

Here, *andhantamah* means blinding darkness. Who will land up in such blinding darkness? Those who practice avidya will. Here *avidya* means, that which is not *vidya* (knowledge) i.e, *karma* . For, it is against knowledge. These are the ones who practice only *karma* in the form of *agnihotra (yaga)* etc. Those who discard *karma* (performance) but engage themselves only in the knowledge of deities, will land themselves up in even severe blinding darkness.

The difference in the intermediary benefits of the paths of *Vidya* (knowledge) and *Karma* (performance) are told here to explain their combination. As otherwise, those bearing fruits and those that would not, would have become main and its supplementary.

Raamaanujeeya : एवं विचित्रशक्तिकपरमात्मविषयां कर्मयोगा-द्यङ्गिकां विद्यामुपदिश्य अनन्तरं त्रिभिर्मन्त्रैः केवलकर्मावलम्बिनः केवलविद्यावलम्बिनश्च पुरुषान्विनिन्दन्वर्णाश्रमधर्मानुगृहीतया विद्ययैव निःश्रेयसावाप्तिं आह -

The intial mantras explained the knowledge of the exceptionally powerful God, which forms part of *karmayoga* . Now, Upanishat criticizes those who follow only the path of karma or only the path of *jnaana* , through three mantras and says the only way to achieve *moksha* is through *jnaana* backed by performance of ordained duties -

बृहदारण्यके चायं मन्त्रः पठितः । ये भोगैश्वर्यप्रसक्ता अविद्या विद्यान्यां क्रियां केवलं कर्मेत्यर्थः । विद्याविधुरं कर्मेति यावत् । अविद्या कर्मसंज्ञाऽन्येति स्मृतेः । उपासते । अनुतिष्ठन्ति । अन्धं तमोऽतिगाढं तमोऽज्ञानमित्यर्थः। त्रिवर्गाभिसङ्गान्नान्तरीयं नरकमन्धं तमो वा । "प्लवा ह्येते अदृढा यज्ञरूपा अष्टादशोक्तमवरं येषु कर्म । एतच्छ्रेयो येऽभिनन्दन्ति मूढा जरामृत्युं ते पुनरेवापि यन्ति" इति श्रुतेः । य उ विद्यायां रताः । उकार उत्तरपदेनान्वेतव्यः । स्वाधिकारोचितकर्म-परित्यागेन विद्यायामेव रताः । ते ततः कर्ममात्रनिष्ठाः प्राप्यादन्ध-तमसाद् भूय इव तमस्तदधिकमज्ञानं प्रविशन्ति । इवशब्दस्तमस इयत्ताया दुर्ग्रहत्वं द्योतयति ॥९॥

Brihadaaranyaka Upanishat also has the same *mantra* . The word *avidya* refers to that knowledge, which deals with the material aspects and their enjoyment. It is interpreted here to mean *karma* , which is other than *vidya* . Rather it is *karma* in isolation, without the accompaniment of *vidya* . He who is engaged in material pleasures and stays only in the performance of *karma*, would go to *andham tamah* – the blinding *ajnaana* , ignorance. The expression can also mean the pitch dark hell that is inseparably associated with *trivarga* (the collective name for *dharma, artha* and *kaama*). Veda says "for those who consider *karma* in the form of eighteen modes of worship (*aasanam, swaagatam, paadyam, arghyam, aachamaneeyakam, snaanam, vastropaveetam, bhooshanaani, gandhah, pushpam, dhoopah, deepah, annam, tarpanam, maalyam, anulepanam, namaskaarah, visarjanam*) as inferior, *Yajnas* are weak boats for them. Those who consider these as their welfare, such fools will get back to this world of aging and death.

Those who are engaged only in *vidya* , i.e., those who have discarded the tasks prescribed by the scripts, would go to deeper hells than what the aforesaid ones engaged only in karma would achieve. The word “ *iva* ” that generally signifies a likening, is meant here to denote the unfathomable depth of *Tamas* .

Madhwaachaarya : अन्यथोपासका ये तु तमोऽन्धं यान्त्यसंशयम् । ततोऽधिकमिव व्यक्तं यान्ति तेषामनिन्दकाः । तस्माद्यथास्वरूपं तु नारायणमनामयम् । अयथार्थस्य निन्दा च (९॥१०) ये विदुस्सह सज्जनाः ।

Quotes from *Koorma puraana* (as commentary for this and the subsequent 5 mantras):

There is no doubt that those who adopt the wrongful path will land up in the world of blinding darkness. But those who do not criticize those in the wrongful path will go to the still worse destinations. Hence he alone is a pious gentleman who knows the true nature of flawless God (*Naaraayana*) and also decries the wrongful knowledge.

It is very much in order to criticize the wrongful knowledge. Not only that criticism is in order, but also is the need, in as much as that of having proper knowledge.

अन्यदेवाहुर्विद्यया

अन्यदेवाहुर्विद्यया अन्यदाहुरविद्यया ।

इति शुश्रुम धीराणां ये नस्तद्विचचक्षिरे ॥ १० ॥

anyadevaahur-vidyayaa anyadaahur-avidyayaa |

iti SuSruma dheeraaNaam ye nastad-vichachaksire |10|

Sankaraachaarya : अन्यत् पृथगेव विद्यया क्रियते फलमिति आहुः वदन्ति, अन्यदाहुरविद्यया कर्मणा क्रियते फलमिति । तथोक्तम् - "कर्मणा पितृलोकः, विद्यया देवलोकः" (बृ. उ. १ । ५ । १६) इति । इति एवं शुश्रुम श्रुतवन्तो वयं धीराणां धीमतां वचनम् । ये आचार्या नः अस्मभ्यं तत् कर्म च ज्ञानं च विचचक्षिरे व्याख्यातवन्तः, तेषामयमागमः पारम्पर्यागत इत्यर्थः ॥

The fruits of knowledge and performance are different. Vedas say that knowledge brings us the divine worlds. The path of performance, referred to here as avidya brings us *pitr loka* , the world of deities representing the departed ancestors. We learn this from the words of the learned. The teachers who taught us the paths of *vidya* and *karma* have explained this concept. Thus it is a perpetrated knowledge.

Raamaanujeeya : किं तर्हि मोक्षसाधनमित्यत्राऽऽह-What then is the means for moksha? Upanishat replies -

विद्ययेति पञ्चम्यर्थे तृतीया । यथाश्रुतेऽन्यशब्दानन्वयादन्यदेवाहुः संभवादिति वक्ष्यमाणानुरोधाच्च । तथा च विद्यायाः कर्मरहित विद्यातोऽन्यन्मोक्षसाधनमित्याहुः । उपनिषद् इति शेषः । अविद्यया । अविद्यायाः । ब्रह्मविद्याविधुरकर्मणोऽन्यदेव मोक्षसाधनमित्याहुः । पूर्वपूर्वसंप्रदायसिद्धोऽयमर्थो अस्माकमित्याह - इति शुश्रुम इति । ये पूर्वाचार्यास्ते प्रणिपातादिभिः सम्यगुपसन्नानामस्माकं तन्मोक्षसाधनं विचचक्षिरे विविध्योपदिदिशुः । तेषां धीराणां धीमतां परमात्मध्यान-पराणां वचनमित्यध्याहार्यम् । यद्वा धीराणामिति पञ्चम्यर्थे षष्ठी । तेभ्यो धीरेभ्य इति योज्यम् । नटस्य शृणोतीतिवत् । इति शुश्रुमः । एवंप्रकारमश्रौषम् । ननु परोक्ष एवार्थे लिङ्विधानाच्छुश्रुमेत्युत्तम-

पुरुषो न घटते इति चेत्सत्यम् । ब्रह्मविद्यायां दुरवगाहत्वेन निःशेष-ग्रहणमस्माभिर्न कृतमित्यभिप्रायकत्वादुत्तमपुरुषप्रयोगस्येत्याहुः ।

The word " *vidyayaa* " should be read in conjunction with " *anyat* " (to mean - different from *vidya*) and not in isolation to mean *vidya* as a tool. As otherwise, it would contradict the usage in the subsequent mantra that says " *anyadaahuh sambhavaat* ". Thus the mantra means – The means to achive moksha is different from vidya that is not accompanied by *karma* . The word " *upanishat* " needs to be imported to complete the meaning "so says upanishat".

Similarly, the means to achieve *moksha* is different from *karma* , which is not accompanied by *brahma vidya* . The *mantra* also indicates that this fact is understood by the ancestors, through the usage of word " *sushruma* " (have been hearing). The gurus have preached these means of securing *moksha* , in detail to us who have sought their guidance after prostrating etc to them. These are the words of such great gurus who have immersed in meditating God. It can also be understood to mean "we have understood from these gurus". In this case the word " *dheeraanaam* " that means something belonging to dheeras – gurus should be understood as the source to mean "from gurus". Since the subject matter of brahma vidya is tough to be understood in whole, the word " *sushrumah* " is presented, to signify the same, in an unusual format that generally is used to communicate an indirect expression.

Madhwaachaarya : ते निन्दयाऽयथार्थस्य दु:खाज्ञानादिरूपिण: । दु:खाज्ञानादिसन्तीर्णा: सुखज्ञानादिरूपिणः ।

By condemning *ayathaartha* that is in the form of sorrow, wrongful knowledge etc, one tides over their effects of sorrow and wrongful knowledge. By practicing the proper knowledge, he would achieve knowledge of God and eternal pleasure.

Criticism of wrongful knowledge is not just because the practice of wrongful knowledge has devastating results. It is also because its criticism bears a different fruit from the one brought by the proper knowledge. Practice of proper knowledge and Criticism of wrongful knowledge fetch us two different components (absence of pain and enjoyment of pleasure) of the ultimate moksha, the salvation

विद्यां चाविद्यां च

विद्यां चाविद्यां च यस्तद्वेदोभयं सह ।

अविद्यया मृत्युं तीर्त्वा विद्ययामृतमश्नुते ॥ ११ ॥

vidyaancha-avidyaancha yastad-vedobham sah |

avidyayaa mrityuṃ teertvaa vidyaya-amritam-aSnute |11|

Sankaraachaarya : यत एवमतः विद्यां च अविद्यां च देवताज्ञानं कर्म चेत्यर्थः । यस्तत् एतदुभयं सह एकेन पुरुषेण अनुष्ठेयं वेद तस्यैवं समुच्चयकारिण एकैकपुरुषार्थसम्बन्धः क्रमेण स्यादित्युच्यते -

Thus whoever understands that both the paths of divine knowledge and performance shall be adopted by the same individual, he will gradually, through their combination, obtain the comprehensive fruits of *purushaartha* , one by one.

अविद्यया कर्मणा अग्निहोत्रादिना मृत्युम् , स्वाभाविकं कर्म ज्ञानं च मृत्युशब्दवाच्यम् , तदुभयं तीर्त्वा अतिक्रम्य विद्यया देवताज्ञानेन अमृतं देवतात्मभावम् अश्नुते प्राप्नोति । तद्ध्यमृतमुच्यते, यद्देवतात्मगमनम् ॥

Through the path of *avidya* (meaning *karma*), the performance of prescribed tasks like agnihotra (sacrifices) one surpasses the natural knowledge and karma, both of which are known as "death". And with the divine knowledge, he achieves divinity (becomes a deity). This achievement of divinity is called *amrita* , salvation.

Raamaanujeeya : अन्यदिति सामान्येनोक्तं मोक्षसाधनं विवृणोति -Whatever has been told as "something different" as a means to achieve *moksha* is explained here:

कुर्वन्नेवेह कर्माणीति मन्त्रे कर्मयोगस्य प्रत्यगात्मदर्शनद्वारा परभक्त्युत्पादकत्वमुक्तम् । इह भक्तियोगेन विदुषा पूर्वोक्तकर्म-योगवेषं परित्यज्याहरहरनुष्ठीयमानानां नित्यनैमित्तिककर्मणां कल्मषनिर्वहणद्वारा भक्त्युपचायकत्वमुच्यते । सहशब्दस्वारस्यात् । अतो न पुनरुक्तता । यो यथावस्थितविद्योपदेशवान् । विद्यां ब्रह्मोपासनरूपां तदङ्गभूतकर्मरूपामविद्यां चैतदुभयं सह वेद । अङ्गाङ्गिभावेन सहानुष्ठेयं वेदेत्यर्थः । अविद्यया विद्याङ्गतया चोदितेन कर्मणा मृत्युं विद्योत्पत्तिप्रतिबन्धकीभूतं पुण्यपापरूपं प्राक्तनकर्म तीर्त्वा निर्विशेषमुल्लङ्ध्य । विद्यया परमात्मोपासनरुपया । अमृतमश्नुते मोक्षं प्राप्नोतीत्यर्थः । तीर्त्वा इत्यत्रोपायविरोधितरणमुच्यते । अमृतमश्नुत इत्युपेयब्रह्मप्राप्तिविरोधिभूतेभ्यः सर्वपापेम्यो मोक्ष इति भेदः । एवं च सति-

इयाज सोऽपि सुबहून्यज्ञाञ्ज्ञानव्यपाश्रयः ।
ब्रह्मविद्यामधिष्ठाय तर्तुं मृत्युमविद्यया ॥ इति ।

ज्ञानव्यपाश्रयः शास्त्रश्रवणजन्यब्रह्मज्ञानवान्स जनकोऽपि ब्रह्मविद्यां निदिध्यासनरूपामधिष्ठाय फलत्वेनाऽऽश्रित्येत्यर्थः । भक्तियोगोत्पत्तिं कामयमान इति यावत् । मृत्युं मत्युत्पत्तिविरोधि प्राचीनं कर्मजातम् । अविद्यया विद्याङ्गकर्मणा तर्तुं व्यपोहितुं सुबहून्यज्ञाञ्ज्योतिष्टोमा-दिकानियाजाकरोत् । पाकं पचतीतिवत् ॥ ११ ॥

In the second mantra, it has been told that *karma yoga* leads to generation of highest *bhakti* through the *darshan* (physical seeing) of God. This mantra speaks of how a *jnaani* discards his earlier role of *karma yoga* and purifies himself through his daily chores and achieves thereby an enhanced level of *bhakti* . This meaning is derived due to the presence of the word " *saha* " in the mantra.

One who has the proper upadesha (preaching) of rightful knowledge – the *jnaana* of *Brahma* and also its component *karma* , the *avidya* and also knows the whole-component relationship between *jnaana* and *karma* and that they need to be practiced together, would through *avidya* – *karma* yoga, cross the hurdle of *punya* and *paapa* (the results of past actions) in the path of acquiring *jnaana* and achieve *moksha* through *vidya* – *upaasana* (deep meditation) of God.

The word " *teertvaa* " signifies overcoming the hurdles that existed in securing the means (tools) and the words " *amritam asnute* " speak of the hurdles existed in the form of *punya* and *paapa* in securing the end (results), the attainment of *brahma praapti* (*moksha*).

The quoted verse speaks of how king Janaka, though a *jnaani* himself continued with meditation and performed many a *yajna* for achieving *bhakti yoga* . He did it so to overcome the accumulated *karma* that stood as a hurdle in achieving *bhakti yoga* .

Madhwaachaarya : यथार्थस्य परिज्ञानात्सुखज्ञानादिरूपताम् । यान्ति

Proper knowledge fetches salvation that is characterized by pleasure and knowledge. One overcomes the misery, symbolically expressed as death through the acts of criticism of improper knowledge and achieves salvation through the practice of proper knowledge.

येऽसम्भूतिमुपासते

अन्धं तमः प्रविशन्ति येऽसम्भूतिमुपासते ।

ततो भूय इव ते तमो य उ सम्भूत्यां रताः ॥ १२॥

andhantamah praviSanti ye asambhootim upaasate |

tato bhooya iva te tamo ya vu sambhootyaagm rataah |12|

Sankaraachaarya : अधुना व्याकृताव्याकृतोपासनयोः समुच्चिचीषया प्रत्येकं निन्दोच्यते - अन्धं तमः प्रविशन्ति ये असम्भूतिम् , सम्भवनं सम्भूतिः सा यस्य कार्यस्य सा सम्भूतिः तस्या अन्या असम्भूतिः प्रकृतिः कारणम् अव्याकृताख्यम् , तामसम्भूतिमव्याकृताख्यां प्रकृतिं कारणमविद्यां कामकर्मबीज-भूतामदर्शनात्मिकाम् उपासते ये ते तदनुरूपमेवान्धं तमः अदर्शनात्मकं प्रविशन्ति । ततः तस्मादपि भूयो बहुतरमिव तमः ते प्रविशन्ति ये उ सम्भूत्यां कार्यब्रह्मणि हिरण्यगर्भाख्ये रताः ॥

Now, with an intent to emphasize on a collective performance of *vyaakrita* and *avyaakrita* upaasana, upanishat criticizes their performance in isolation-

That which has a cause (for its creation) is called *sambhooti* , the born. The one that does not have a cause is *asambhooti* . This is *prakriti* , the minutest form of matter and is known as *avyaakrita* and *avidyaa* , the wrongful knowledge. This is the root cause of all material desires and actions in quest of them. He, who worships this *avyaakrita* , subtle matter that forms the seed of all material desires and is invisible, will accordingly enter the blinding darkness. The one who worships *kaarya brahma* , (the deity with four heads and is popularly known as the creator of the universe) also known as *Hiranyagarbha* , will enter the still darker worlds.

Raamaanujeeya : एवं समाधिनिष्पत्तेर्नित्यनैमित्तिककर्मसाध्य-त्वमुक्त्वाऽथ त्रिभिर्मन्त्रैः निषिद्धनिवृत्तिरूपयोगाङ्गसाध्यत्वमाह - तत्र तावत्प्राग्वदेकैकमात्रं विनिन्दति -

Having thus narrated the performance of ordained daily duties as a means to achieve *samaadhi* , Upanishat now explains that part of yoga, which speaks of how to distance from the prohibited aspects, through the next three mantras. Even here, like in the earlier ones, performance of any one in isolation is only criticized.

"एतमितः प्रेत्याभिसंभविताऽस्मि" (छा.उ. ३।१४।४।) "ब्रह्मलोकम-भिसंभवामि (छा.उ. ८।१३।१) इत्यादिषु ब्रह्मप्राप्तिरूपाऽनुभूतिः संभूतिशब्देनोक्ता । इह तु समाधिरूपा संभूतिशब्देनोच्यते । असंभूतिशब्दस्तु समाध्यङ्गभूतां निषिद्धनिवृत्तिमाह । संभूतिं च विनाशं चेत्युत्तरत्र विनाशशब्देनासंभूतेरनुविधानात् । तथा च ये विद्याधिकारिणोऽसंभूतिमेव मानदम्भहिंसास्तेयादीनां योगविरुद्धानां निवृत्तिमेवोपासते निवृत्तिमात्रनिष्ठा इत्यर्थः । तेऽन्धं तमः प्रविशन्तीति पूर्ववदर्थः । ये पुनः समाधिरूपसंभूत्यामेव रतास्ते ततो भूय इव तमः प्रविशन्तीत्यर्थः ॥१२॥

Based on the usage as in " *etam itah pretya abhisam-bhavitaa asmi* - I would join this person after departing from here". " *brahmalokam abhisambhavaami* - I will enter brahma loka", the word " *sambhooti* " is understood to mean the experience of joining *Brahma* . However here, it is taken to mean *samaadhi* – deep meditation. The word *asambhooti* means that component of *samaadhi* which constitutes discarding of prohibited actions. This is because in the subsequent mantra the word " *vinaasha* " is used to indicate " *asambhooti* ".

Thus the mantra means – those who are eligible for vidya and practice only removal of *asambhooti* – the hurdles of yoga comprising of *maana* (pride – feeling oneself as great), *damba* (arrogance), *ahimha* (non-voilence), *astheya* (not taking some ones property) etc , they would enter andha tamas. On the other hand those who do not practice these things but perform only *samaadhi* , they enter even deeper *andha tamas* .

Madhwaachaarya : एवं सृष्टिकर्तृत्वं नाङ्गीकुर्वन्ति ये हरेः । तेऽपि यान्ति तमो घोरं तथा संहारकर्तृताम् ।

Similar to what has been told with reference to the practice of wrongful knowledge, the one who does not accept God as the creator of this universe, will go to the dark worlds called *andha tamas* . Those who do not accept God as the destructor (who profess that God is only the creator but not the destructor) will land themselves up in still darker worlds.

अन्यदेवाहुः सम्भवात्

अन्यदेवाहुः सम्भवादन्यदाहुरसम्भवात् ।

इति शुश्रुम धीराणां ये नस्तद्विचचक्षिरे ॥ १३ ॥

anyadevaahus-sambhavaad anyadaahur-asambhavaat |

iti SuSruma dheeraaNaam ye nastad-vichachakshire |13|

Sankaraachaarya : अधुना उभयोरुपासनयोः समुच्चय-कारणमवयवफलभेदमाह -

Now, the difference in results of practicing two different paths are explained.

अन्यदेव पृथगेव आहुः फलं सम्भवात् सम्भूतेः कार्यब्रह्मोपासनात् अणिमाद्यैश्वर्यलक्षणम् आख्यातवन्त इत्यर्थः । तथा च अन्यदाहुरसम्भवात् असम्भूतेः अव्याकृतात् अव्याकृतोपासनात् यदुक्तम् "अन्धं तमः प्रविशन्ति" (ई. उ. ९) इति, प्रकृतिलय इति च पौराणिकैरुच्यते । इति एवं शुश्रुम धीराणां वचनं ये नः तद्विचचक्षिरे व्याकृताव्याकृतोपासनफलं व्याख्यातवन्त इत्यर्थः ॥

The fruits of worshiping *kaaryabrahma* are different. They are, begetting the extraordinary powers like condensing oneself to a miniature size or growing to a huge size etc. Those who practice the path of *avyakrta* , the un-manifest matter, will go to the dark worlds. This is also called as " *prakriti laya* ". We learn this from the words of the learned persons and through *puraaNas* .

Raamaanujeeya : किं तर्हि मोक्षसाधनमित्यत्राऽऽह-

What then is the means to achieve *moksha* ? -

संभवात्संभूतेः । असंभवादसंभूतेरित्यर्थः । केवलात्संभवादसंभवा-च्चान्यदेव मोक्षसाधनमित्युपनिषद आहुः। लिङुत्तमः पूर्ववत् । शिष्टं स्पष्टम् ॥ १३॥

Performance of only *sambhooti* and only *asambhooti* have results other than moksha. The usage of first person, "we learn" is as in the previous mantra. The meaning of the remaining words are clear.

Madhwaachaarya : नाङ्गीकुर्वन्ति तेऽप्येवं तस्मात् सर्वगुणात्मकम् । सर्वकर्तारमीशेशं सर्वसंहारकारणम् ॥१३॥

Thus, those who do not accept God as full of all qualities, as the creator of everything, as the lord of all lords, as the destructor of everything will enter the dark or darker worlds as described above – Those who do not accept God as the creator would land in *andha tamas* and those who consider him to be only the creator and not the destructor would land in deeper *andha tamas* .

सम्भूतिं च विनाशं च

सम्भूतिं च विनाशं च यस्तद्वेदोभयं सह ।

विनाशेन मृत्युं तीर्त्वा सम्भूत्यामृतमश्नुते ॥ १४॥

sambhootim cha vinaaSam cha yastad-vedobhayagm saha |

vinaaSena mrityum teertvaa sambhootya-amritamaSnute |14|

<u>Sankaraachaarya</u> : यत एवम् , अतः समुच्चयः सम्भूत्यसम्भूत्युपासनयोर्युक्तः एकैकपुरुषार्थत्वाच्चेत्याह -

सम्भूतिं च विनाशं च यस्तद्वेदोभयं सह, विनाशेन, विनाशो धर्मो यस्य कार्यस्य स तेन धर्मिणा अभेदेनोच्यते "विनाशः" इति । तेन तदुपासनेनानैश्वर्यमधर्मकामादिदोषजातं च मृत्युं तीर्त्वा, हिरण्य-गर्भोपासनेन ह्यणिमादिप्राप्तिः फलम् , तेनानैश्वर्यादिमृत्युमतीत्य, असम्भूत्या अव्याकृतोपासनया अमृतं प्रकृतिलयलक्षणम् अश्नुते ।

Since it is so, a combined upaasana of sambhooti and asambhooti should be done. This is also true since they facilitate only one *purushaartha* (desired results) individually.

This explains the impact of two things viz. *sambhooti* (Creation) and *vinaaSa* (Destruction). Anything which is destructible by its very nature is referred to here as *vinaaSa* . He, who practices (believes) in achieving these perishables, surpasses the death, a resultant of the inglorious set of flaws like the desire for the forbidden and achieves, on account of worshiping *hiranyagarbha* , the special prowess of *aNima* (The capacity to shrink oneself to a minute size) etc. However, the one who practices *asambhooti* , the unmanifest, will achieve the eternity that is characterized by the detachment from the matter.

"सम्भूतिं च विनाशं च" इत्यत्रावर्णलोपेन निर्देशो द्रष्टव्यः, प्रकृतिलयफलश्रुत्यनुरोधात् ॥

The absence of essential letter 'a' in " *sambhootim* " and " *vinaaSam* " is indicative of the loss / detachment of matter as the fruit of the aforesaid worship/practice.

मानुषदैववित्तसाध्यं फलं शास्त्रलक्षणं प्रकृतिलयान्तम् ; एतावती संसारगतिः । अतः परं पूर्वोक्तम् "आत्मैवाभूद्विजानतः" इति सर्वात्मभाव एव सर्वैषणासंन्यासज्ञाननिष्ठाफलम् । एवं द्विप्रकारः प्रवृत्तिनिवृत्तिलक्षणो वेदार्थोऽत्र प्रकाशितः । तत्र प्रवृत्तिलक्षणस्य वेदार्थस्य विधिप्रतिषेधलक्षणस्य कृत्स्नस्य प्रकाशने प्रवर्ग्यान्तं ब्राह्मणमुपयुक्तम् । निवृत्तिलक्षणस्य प्रकाशने अत ऊर्ध्वं बृहदारण्यकम् ।

Anything that is quoted in the scripts as achievable with the help of human or divine resources, does not extend beyond the time when matter gets disintegrated. The world, the cycle of births and deaths also cannot move beyond this. What surpasses this limit is the concept of sarvaatma, the oneness of everything with God. This is the resultant of renouncement of all desires and progression in the path of knowledge as preached in the previous mantra, *aatmaivaabhoot* ... Thus the two paths of progress *pravritti* and *nivritti* that are explained in vedas are made known here. The initial part of *Brihadaaranyaka upanishat* upto the stage of " *pravargya* " explains the pravritti path. Its subsequent part deals with *nivritti* path.

तत्र निषेकादिश्मशानान्तं कर्म कुर्वन् जिजीविषेद्यो विद्यया सहापरब्रह्मविषयया, तदुक्तम् - "विद्यां चाविद्यां च यस्तद्वेदोभयं सह । अविद्यया मृत्युं तीर्त्वा विद्ययामृतमश्नुते" (ई. उ. ११) इति,

Thus the discussion on the practice of *vidya* and *avidya* etc., is meant for those who have a desire to live their entire life, right from the conception in their mothers' womb till their last breath through performance of karma. The term *vidya* in this context refers to the knowledge of *aparabrahma* . This has been told in the earlier mantra " *vidyaam chaavidyaam cha. .*".

Raamaanujeeya : अन्यदित्युक्तं विवृणोति-

संभूतिं समाधिरूपब्रह्मानुभूतिं विनाशं च योगविरोधिनां वर्जनं चेत्येतदुभयं यो विद्वानङ्गाङ्गिभावेन सह वेद स विद्वान्विनाशेन निषेव्यमाणेनेति शेषः। विरोधिनिवृत्तिरूपयोगाङ्गसेवनेनेत्यर्थः। मृत्युं समाधिविरोधिपापं तीर्वाऽपाकृत्य निष्पन्नया संभूत्याऽमृतमश्नुते ब्रह्मप्राप्तिरूपां संभूतिमश्नुत इति भावः। अत्र संभूतिविनाशशब्दाभ्यां सृष्टिप्रलयविवक्षया कार्यहिरण्यगर्भस्याव्याकृतप्रधानस्योपासनं विधीयते इति शांकरं व्याख्यानमनुपपन्नम्। मृत्युतरणामृतत्वप्राप्ति-रूपफलविधानानौचित्यात् ॥१४॥

That wise person who considers sambhooti, the experience of *Brahma* in *samaadhi* and *vinaasham* , the deterrence from stealth and violence as complementary to each other and practices them both, he would overcome the obstacles of *paapa* , sin through *vinaasha* and achieve sambhooti in the form of attainment of *moksha* through *sambhooti* , the deep meditation.

The meaning of sambhooti and *vinaasha* as construed by *Sankara* in his commentary as "creation and destruction", "upaasana of *Hiranyagarbha* and *pradhaana* (the core matter)" is inappropriate. For, the benefits of crossing the *samsaara* and achieving *moksha* as narrated by upanishat would not fit in with such an interpretation.

Madhwaachaarya : यो वेद संहृतिज्ञानात् देहबन्धाद्विमुच्यते। सुखज्ञानादिकर्तृत्वज्ञानात्तद् व्यक्तिमाव्रजेत्। सर्वदोषविनिर्मुक्तं गुणरूपं जनार्दनम्। जानीयान्न गुणानां च भागहानिं प्रकल्पयेत्। न मुक्तानामपि हरेस्साम्यं विष्णोरभिन्नताम्। नैव प्रचिन्तयेत् तस्माद्ब्रह्मादेस्साम्यमेव वा मानुषादिविरिञ्चान्तं तारतम्यं विमुक्तिगम्। ततो विष्णोः परोत्कर्षं सम्यग्ज्ञात्वा विमुच्यते इति कौर्मे ॥१४॥

Thus he who understands God as the destructor will get released from the cycle of births and deaths. Similarly, the inherent qualities like pleasure and knowledge get manifested on account of knowing that God as the creator of everything including the pleasure and knowledge in every individual. It shall be understood that

1. God (also known by the name *Janaardhana*) is devoid of any kind of defect or negative qualities,

2. He is the embodiment of all good qualities,

3. None of his good qualities are fractional (each one is complete and unlimited), that even after salvation no one can be equal to him or become one with him,

4. He shall never be understood as equal to anyone including *Chaturmukha* , the supreme amongst deities,

5. All beings, right from the humans to *Chaturmukha* have a hierarchical gradation even after their attainment of *moksha* ,

6. God (also known by the name *ViShnu*) is the supreme most at all times.

By understanding the above, one will achieve moksha, salvation.

All the above (presented as commentary for the mantras 9, 10,11,12, 13 and 14) are quoted from *Koorma puraaNa.* (*Madhwacharya* has a typical style of just quoting from the ancient texts as commentary for the mantras. He adds a word or two only if the quotes need an explanation for better clarity. Here the quoted texts are unambiguous and hence he has not put any additional explanation. It is often surprising that *puraaNas* have some of their contents that typically look like commentaries to the tough Upanishats).

हिरण्मयेन पात्रेण

हिरण्मयेन पात्रेण सत्यस्यापिहितं मुखम् ।

तत्त्वं पूषन्नपावृणु सत्यधर्माय दृष्टये ॥ १५ ॥

hiraNmayena paatreNa satyasyaapihitam mukham |

tatvam pooShannapaavriNu satyadharmaaya driShtaye |15|

<u>Sankaraachaarya</u> : तत्र सोऽधिकारी केन मार्गेणामृतत्वम् अश्नुते इत्युच्यते - "तद्यत्तत्सत्यमसौ स आदित्यो य एष एतस्मिन्मण्डले पुरुषो यश्चायं दक्षिणेऽक्षन्पुरुषः" (बृ. उ. ५ । ५ । २) एतदुभयं सत्यं ब्रह्मोपासीनः यथोक्तकर्मकृच्च यः, सोऽन्तकाले प्राप्ते सत्यात्मानमात्मनः प्राप्तिद्वारं याचते हिरण्मयेन पात्रेण इति -

The path of salvation is explained here. That which is true is *aaditya* (Sun). The one who is inside this spherical solar object is also Him. He is also found in the right eye of humans. Both of these are true. He who practices the path of *brahma* and also the one who practices prescribed *karma* ultimately prays God for the righteous path of achieving oneness with him. The prayer runs thus:

हिरण्मयमिव हिरण्मयम् , ज्योतिर्मयमित्येतत् , तेन पात्रेणेव अपिधानभूतेन सत्यस्य आदित्यमण्डलस्थस्य ब्रह्मणः अपिहितम् आच्छादितं मुखं द्वारम् ; तत् त्वं हे पूषन् अपावृणु अपसारय सत्यधर्माय तव सत्यस्योपासनात्सत्यं धर्मो यस्य मम सोऽहं सत्यधर्मा तस्मै मह्यम् ; अथवा, यथाभूतस्य धर्मस्यानुष्ठात्रे, दृष्टये तव सत्यात्मन उपलब्धये ॥

That which is very much like *hiranya* , gold, is *hiranmayam* – Luminescent. This (luminous solar aura) is, like a lid of a vessel, blocking the way to God, who is referred to as *satya* , truth who is dwelling inside this solar sphere. O! *pooshan* , please uncover this *aura* to allow me, the one who has inculcated the worship of this Truth, to see Him. Please uncover to facilitate the worship of the Truth by looking at its true form.

Raamaanujeeya : एवं साङ्गभगवद्भक्तिमुपदिश्य तन्निष्ठस्यानुसंधेय-मन्त्रद्वयमुपदिशति -

After thus explaining *bhakti* along with its components, the upanishat now tells about what needs to be borne in mind by those practicing *bhakti* .

हे पूषन्नादित्यान्तर्यामिन्। "य आदित्ये तिष्ठन्नि"त्यारभ्य "य आदित्यमन्तरो यमयति" (३।७।५) इति शतपथश्रुतेः । शास्त्रदृष्ट्या तूपदेशो वामदेववदित्यादिन्यायाच्च । यद्वा पूषन्नाश्रितपोषणस्वभावेत्यर्थः। "साक्षादप्यविरोधं जैमिनिः (ब्र. सू. १।२।२८) इति सूत्रानुरोधात् । सत्यस्य। सत्यशब्देन स्वरुपविकाररहितजीवात्मोच्यते। "सत्यं चानृतं च सत्यमभवदि"त्यादिषु (छा.उ. १।२।३) जीवेऽपि सत्यशब्दप्रयोगात्। तस्य मुखम्। मुखवत्। अनेकेन्द्रियावष्टम्भ-कतया मुखसदृशं मन इत्यर्थः। हिरण्मयेन हिरण्यसदृशेन भोग्यवर्गेण इति यावत्। पात्रेण परमात्मविषयकवृत्तिप्रतिरोधकेनापिहितम् आच्छादितम्। हृदि निहिते परमात्मनि निरुद्धवृत्तिकं जातमित्यर्थः। तज्जीवस्य मुखस्थानीयं मनो हृषीकाणामीशस्त्वमपावृणु निरस्य तिरोधानं कुर्वित्यर्थः। तत्कस्य, हेतोस्तत्राऽऽह - सत्यधर्माय सत्यस्य जीवस्य धर्मभूताय। दृष्टिदर्शनम्। त्वद्दर्शनायेति भावः ॥ १५ ॥

Pooshan - one who stays in Sun and regulates him. *Shatapatha* text of vedas provides this meaning through its mantras from "he who stays in Sun" to "he who regulates Sun from within". *Brahma Sutra* (1-1-30) says that God is in everyone as a regulator. Another meaning of " *pooshan* " is that he is the guardian of those who seek shelter under him. This is also in accordance with the sutra (1-2-28) where it says the words that address others in usage also speak of *Brahma* in their primary sense without any conflict. The mind of *jeeva* is covered by the material pleasures. O! *Pooshan* , kindly lift it to facilitate a glimpse of you for the benefit of him, who is in the path of *satya* and *dharma* .

The word " *satya* " is taken to mean *jeeva* who is innately immutable. In *Chandogya Upanishat* , it is said that " *satyam cha anritam cha satyamabhavat* ". The word " *mukha* " that generally means face, is taken here to mean the mind because it is like the face of all *indriyas* . The word " *hiranmaya* " would normally means golden. However it is taken here to mean the entire of material pleasures as a group that is attractive like gold. This is blocking the view of God who is very much inside the heart. Though " *paatra* " would mean a plate or vessel, it is taken as an obstacle / veil that is preventing an approach to God.

Madhwaachaarya : पात्रं हिरण्मयं सूर्यमण्डलं समुदाहृतम् । विष्णोस्सत्यस्य तेनैव सर्वदाऽपिहितं मुखम् । तत्तु पूर्णत्वत: पूषा विष्णुर्दर्शयति स्वयम् । सत्यधर्माय भक्ताय (१५) प्रधानज्ञानरूपतः।

Quotes from *BrahmaaNDa Puraana:* The solar sphere is referred to as the golden plate. The face of *Vishnu* , also referred to as *Satya* is always covered by this plate. *Vishnu* is called *poosha* meaning "the complete" because he is the embodiment of knowledge. He only will exhibit his face to his devotees who are in the righteous path.

Thus, this mantra makes it amply clear that no one can claim witnessing God as a matter of right by virtue of his knowledge, practice of a particular path etc. It is the exclusive privilege of God to make himself visible to whomsoever he desires so to do.

पूषन्नेकर्षे यम

पूषन्नेकर्षे यम सूर्य प्राजापत्य व्यूह रश्मीन्समूह

तेजो यत्ते रूपं कल्याणतमं तत्ते पश्यामि॥१६॥

pooshan ekarShe yama soorya praajaapatya

vyooha raSmeen samooha |

tejo yatte roopam kalyaanatamam tatte paSyaami | 16 |

योऽसावसौ पुरुषः सोऽहमस्मि ॥ १७ ॥

yosavasau puruShassohamasmi |17|

Sankaraachaarya : हे पूषन् जगतः पोषणात्पूषा रविः। तथा एक एव ऋषति गच्छतीत्येकर्षिः हे एकर्षे। तथा सर्वस्य संयमनाद्यमः हे यम। तथा रश्मीनां प्राणानां रसानां च स्वीकरणात्सूर्यः हे सूर्य। प्रजापतेरपत्यं प्राजापत्यः हे प्राजापत्य। व्यूह विगमय रश्मीन् स्वान्। समूह एकीकुरु उपसंहर तेजः तावकं ज्योतिः।

O! *Pooshan* , Sun. Sun is called *pooshan* since he does *poshaNa* (provides food) of the world. O! *ekarshi* , the one who moves in solitude. O! yama, the regulator. O! *soorya* , the one who sucks in lives and liquids. O! *praajaapatya* , son of prajaapati. Remove thy rays, bundle them up. Subside the high glow.

यत् ते तव रूपं कल्याणतमम् अत्यन्तशोभनम्, तत् ते तवात्मनः प्रसादात् पश्यामि। किञ्च, अहं न तु त्वां भृत्यवद्याचे योऽसौ आदित्यमण्डलस्थः असौ व्याहृत्यवयवः पुरुषः पुरुषाकारत्वात्, पूर्णं वानेन प्राणबुद्ध्यात्मना जगत्समस्तमिति पुरुषः; पुरि शयनाद्वा पुरुषः। सोऽहम् अस्मि भवामि॥

I would like to see your most sacred form by your grace. But I do not beg like a servant. The one who is inside the glorious solar aura, who is in the human form but complete (*purushah* – one who stays in bodies), who has *vyaahriti* (*om*) as his body, who is this entire world inclusive of the living and intelligent beings, is me and remains so.

Raamaanujeeya : पुनरपि तया दृष्ट्या दृष्टव्यं विशिंषन्दर्शनं तत्साधनं चाभ्यर्थयते -

Prays again through further description of the intended and the means thereof.

पूषन्नाश्रितपोषक । एकश्चासावृषिश्चैकर्षिः । अद्वितीयातीन्द्रियार्थद्रष्टा । "नान्योऽतोऽस्ति द्रष्टा" (बृ.उ.३०।७।२३) इति श्रुतेः । यमो यमयति सर्वानिति यमः। सर्वान्तर्यामिन् । "यः पृथिवीमन्तरो यमयति" (बृ.उ.३।७।३) "य आत्मानमन्तरो यमयति" (बृ.उ. ३।७।९) इत्यादिश्रुतेः । सूर्य स्वोपासकधियां सुष्टु प्रेरक। प्राजापत्य प्रजापतिश्चतुर्मुखस्तस्य सुताः प्राजापत्यास्तेषामन्तर्यामिन् । यद्वा प्रजापतिरेव प्राजापत्यः । प्रजानांपतिरिति व्युत्पत्त्या प्रजापतिर्विष्णुः "प्रजापतिश्चरति गर्भे अन्तः" (म. ना.१।१) इति श्रुतेः ।

Pooshan – Guardian of those who have surrendered.

Ekarshe – One with an unparalleled vision of invisible aspects. Sruti says, there is no one else who has a vision.

Yama – One who regulates everything by staying within them. Brihadaaranyaka Upanishat says – He is the one who regulates Prithivi from within, one who regulates jeevas from within.

Soorya – One who directs the minds of his followers in the proper path.

Praajaapatya – One who stays in and regulates the off springs of *Prajaapati* – *Chaturmukha Brahma* . Also means *Vishnu* , who is the lord of subjects - all beings. This usage is also found in vedas- "prajaapatih charati garbhe antah".

व्यूह रश्मीन् । भवदीयदिव्यरूपदर्शनानुपयुक्तान्स्वोग्ररश्मीन्व्यूह व्यपोह विगमयेत्यर्थः । यत्ते दर्शनोपयिकं प्रभात्मकं तेजस्तत्समूह समूही कुरु । तत्किमर्थमित्याशङ्क्य द्रष्टुमिच्छामि ते रूपमित्याह यदिति यत् । "आदित्यवर्णं तमसः परस्तात् " (श्वे.उ. ३.८) इत्यादिश्रुतिषु प्रसिद्धमित्यर्थः। "आनन्दो ब्रह्म" (तै.उ. ३।६) इति निरतिशयभोग्यस्य तवापि । कल्याणतमं सौन्दर्यादिगुणातिशयेन कल्याणेभ्योऽतिशयितं कल्याणं शुभाश्रयमिति भावः । ते यद्दिव्यरूपं तत्पश्यामि पश्येयमिति लकारव्यत्ययश्छान्दसः । द्रष्टुमिच्छामीति भावः ।

ननु “यत्ते रूपं कल्याणतमम्” । “य एषोऽन्तरादित्ये हिरण्मयः पुरुषः” । (छा.उ. १।६।६) “ईशा वास्यमिदं सर्वम्” (ई.उ.१) “पतिं विश्वस्याऽऽत्मेश्वरम्” (म. ना. २१।३) “सर्वकर्मा सर्वगन्धः । स्वाभाविकी ज्ञानबलक्रिया च” (श्वे.उ.६।८)। “तस्य ह वा एतस्य ब्रह्मणो नाम सत्यमिति” (छा.उ. ८।३।४) “तस्योदिति नाम” (छा.उ. १६७) इत्यादिभिः शास्त्रैर्गुणविग्रहादयो ब्रह्मणो विधीयन्ते । निर्गुणं निरञ्जनम्। “सत्यं ज्ञानम् “ (तै.उ. २।१।१) “अकायमव्रणम् ।” (ई.उ.८) “नेह नानाऽस्ति किंचन” (बृ.उ. ४।४।१९) “निष्कलं निष्क्रियम् (श्वे.उ.६।१९) “अगोत्रमवर्णम्” (मु.उ. १।१।६] एवमादिभिः शास्त्रैर्गुणादयः प्रतिषिध्यन्ते । तथा विधिनिषेधयोः शास्त्रयोर्विरोधात् अन्यतरबाधो अवश्यंभावी। तत्र निषेधस्य प्रसक्ति-पूर्वकतया पश्चात्प्रवृत्तिं प्रतिषेधशास्त्रमपच्छेदाधिकरणन्यायेन प्रबलम् । अतः प्रतिषेधबलेन गुणादिविधयः सर्वे बाधिताः । ततश्च विद्याख्य-दोषपरिकल्पितगुणविग्रहादयो मिथ्याभूता इति । तदिदमनादरणीयम् । पशुच्छागनयेनोत्सर्गापवादनयेन च विधिनिषेधयोर्भिन्नविषयत्वोप-पादनेन तयोर्विरोधगन्धाभावाद्विधीनां प्रतिषेधबाध्यता-नुपपत्तेः । तदुक्तं तत्त्वसारे -

यद्ब्रह्मणो गुणविकारशरीरभेदकर्मादिगोचरविधिप्रतिषेधवाचः ।
अन्योन्यभिन्नविषया न विरोधगन्धमर्हन्ति तन्न विधयः प्रतिषेधबाध्या: ॥ इति ।

O *Pooshan* ! (all the above are his attributes), remove all such hurting rays that form an obstacle in viewing your divine form and bring in those bright rays that facilitate such viewing . For, I have a desire to see this form of yours that is famous in vedic texts like “ *aaditya varnam tamasah parastaat* ”. As told in *Taittareeya Upanishat* , you have unlimited pleasure – *aanando brahma* . Your form is all the more pleasing because of its beauty and other qualities. Hence it is referred to here as *kalyaanatamam* – the superlative expression of *kalyaana* . It is this extraordinary form that I would like to see. The word *kalyaana* has a gross equivalence in English with “good”, “virtuous” etc.

We now have a discussion incidental to the above statement that God has a *kalyana-tamam* body. Some vedic texts describe God as having “ *kalyanatamam* " body, some say “ *hiranmayah* " - Golden. Some other says the entire universe is his body, yet another says "He is the master and soul of the universe". They also describe him to be the doer of all tasks, as the one who is himself all the qualities like *gandha* , as the one who is innately an embodiment of knowledge, strength and action. They also call him *satya* etc. Thus, it is clear that he has a body with lot of positive attributes.

While this is so, some other vedic texts call him *nirgunam* (having no qualities), *niranjanam* (no defects), is just truth and knowledge, has neither a body nor an injury, is one and the only, has neither components nor actions, has neither an ancestry nor a sect etc. Since these are contradictory, only one of the contradicting set can be true – either that he has a body or that he does not have one.

Here, the statements that negate qualities in God are stronger since they are preceded by those assigning qualities and that the maxim (rule of interpretation) in *apacheda adhikarana* supports such a treatment. Hence all qualities that are construed to exist due to the defect of *avidya* are illusory - This argument should not be accepted.

Applying the maxims of *pashuchaga adhikarana* and *utsargaapavaada adhikarana,* the vedic statements that speak of existence and those that speak of an absence of attributes are pointed at different aspects. Hence there is no contradiction.

The *adhikaranas* quoted above are from *poorvameemsa* .

The script " *tatvasaara* " clarifies as under:

The statements that speak of an existence as well as absence of *guna, vikaara, shareera, bheda, karma* etc have different subjects of reference. Hence they do not have even a scent of contradiction. Thus they do not invalidate each other.

अथान्तर्यामिणमहंग्रहेणानुसंधत्ते - योऽसावसौ पुरुषः सोऽहमस्मीति ।

This aspect of God being the *antaryaami* – the internal regulator is emphasized with the word " *aham* " -

यद्यपि - पुरुषं प्रकृतिं चैव प्रधानपुरुषेश्वरः (गी.१३.१९) इत्यादिषु पुरुषशब्दो जीववाचितया प्रसिद्धस्तथाऽपि "तेनेदं पूर्णं पुरुषेण सर्वम्" (श्वे.उ.३९) इत्यादिश्रुत्या सर्ववेदपठितपुरुषसूक्तादिषु प्रसिद्धो महापुरुष एवेह पुरुषशब्देन विवक्षितः । नन्वेवं योऽसौ पुरुषः सोऽहम् इति कथं सामानाधिकरण्यम् । अहंपदार्थस्य जीवस्य महापुरुषाद्भिन्न-त्वादिति चेन्न । अहंशब्देनाप्यस्मदर्थान्तर्यामिण एवाभिधानेनाहं स इति निर्देशस्य सुसंगतत्वात् । ननु चाहंशब्दस्य प्रत्यगर्थान्तर्यामित्वपरत्वे सोऽस्मीत्युत्तमपुरुषो न घटते । नहि तदन्तर्यामिपुरुषोऽस्मीत्यन्वयो युज्यत इति चेदुच्यते - मदन्तर्यामीत्यादिशब्दान्तरेणोपस्थापिते प्रत्यगर्थान्तर्यामिण्युत्तमपुरुषान्वयासंभवेऽपि अहमित्यस्मत्पदोप-स्थापिते तस्मिन्नुत्तमपुरुषान्वयो युज्यत एव । तथा च सूत्रम् - अस्मद्युत्तमः (पा० सू.१।४।१०७) इति । प्रत्यगर्थबोधकास्मच्छब्दोपपद उत्तमपुरुषो भवतीत्यर्थः ।

There is a word " *purusha* " in the above mantra. Though the word refers to *jeeva* as in the usage " *purusham prakritim chaiva pradhaana purusheshwarah* ", it primarily addresses the one who is the subject of *purusha sookta* that figures in all the *vedas* . Now the question is how this *purusha* is considered as one with " *aham* " - "me"? The word aham represents *jeeva* who is certainly different from *Purusha* , God. True. However, the word aham should be understood to mean the one dwelling in me and not just me. There is one more hurdle in this interpretation. The statement " *so aham asm* i - I am him", puts the verb in first person. If the word "I" is to be understood to mean some one present in me, how would the usage of first person fit in? True, the usage of first person may not fit in if the word "I" is replaced by "one within me". It is not so. The statement remains intact with the word "I" and hence the usage of first person as well. However only the intent is shifted from "me" to "one in me". The rule book of Panini's Sanskrit grammar (at 1.4.107) supports this interpretation.

न पुनरस्मच्छब्दस्य प्रत्यगर्थद्वारा परमात्मपर्यन्ततायामुत्तमनिवृत्तिरिति । अधिकं तु प्रविष्टं न तद्धानिरिति न्यायात् । एवं तत्त्वमसीत्यादिष्व-प्यस्तीति मध्यमपुरुषो निर्वाह्यः । त्वंपदेनाभिमुखचेतनद्वारैव तदन्त-र्यामिणोऽभिधानाभ्युपगमात् । तत्रापि "युष्मद्युपपदे समानाधिकरणे स्थानिन्यपि मध्यमः" (पा० सू०१।४।१०५) इत्येतावदेव हि स्मर्यते । न तु युष्मच्छब्दस्य स्वाभिमुखचेतनद्वारा तदन्तर्यामिपर्यन्तत्वे मध्यमनिवृत्तिरिति । ये तु तत्त्वमसि सोऽहमस्मीत्यादिष्वहंत्वमादि-शब्दैर्युष्मदस्मदर्थपरित्यागेन् निर्विशेषचिन्मात्रस्वरूपैक्यमेव वाक्य-वेद्यमित्याहुः, तानेव तत्त्वमसीत्यादिवाक्येष्वसिरिव सोऽहमस्मीति-वाक्यस्थास्मिरपि खण्डयति। श्रोतर्यनुसंधातरि च युष्मदस्मत्ते हि तैः परित्यक्ते न तेषामसिना कश्चित्प्रतिबोधनीयोऽस्ति न च कश्चिदस्मिना विशिष्यानुसंदेहः । ननु प्रकृते युष्मदस्मदोरविवक्षायामपि तयोर्व्युत्पन्न-युष्मद स्मच्छब्दोपपदमात्रोपजीवनेनास्मत्पक्षेऽपि त्वमहम् इति मध्यमोत्तमयोः संपत्तिरिति चेत् । ततोऽप्यपरित्यक्तप्रवृत्तिनिमित्त-कस्यास्माकं निर्वहणस्यैवानुसर्तुमुचितत्वात् ।

By thus interpreting the word ' *aham* ' as "the one who is dwelling in me" and thereby to mean God, the meaning of "me" for that word is not denied. This is only an additional meaning. An addition does not remove the original. Similar approach needs to be had while interpreting other confusing words like *tatvamasi* . Though the word " *tvam* " - "you" is in second person, the word is used to address God who is dwelling in the person standing in front. Hence the meaning of second person (one standing in front) is not discarded. Even this is in accordance with the *Panini* 's grammar rule (at 1.4.105). The irregularity however is in those interpretations where the meaning of "you" and "me" in *tatvamasi* and *sohamasmi* etc is discarded and only the fact of both being *chetana* is taken to mean an unity of God and *jeeva* on the basis of *asi* in *tatvamasi* and *asmi* in *sohamasmi* . If the words "you" and "me" representing the speaker and listener are ignored, then the listener has nothing to learn from the word *asi* nor would *asmi* communicate anything specifically. If it is to be said that the intention in the aforesaid statements is not in speaking of “you” and “me” but of the oneness of those referenced by such words and that only the persons referenced by the said words are considered discarding the sense of first person, second person or third person, even this cannot be accepted. Our interpretation respects the category of first person etc. Hence deserves higher acceptability.

अपर आह योऽसावसौ पुरुषः सोऽहमस्मीत्यत्र पुरुषशब्देन परमपुरुषो न विवक्षणीयः । तथा सत्युत्तमपुरुष इत्याख्यायाः सोऽहमिति सामानाधिकरण्यस्य च लेशेन निर्वाह्यत्वात्। अतो वरमत्र पुरुषशब्दस्य परिशुद्धजीवात्मपरत्वमाश्रयितुम् । एवं च सति यः पुरुषो मुक्तिदृश्यभाव्याकारः परिशुद्धजीवात्मा सोऽहमस्मीत्यन्वयात् उत्तमपुरुष इत्याख्यायाः सामानाधिकरण्यस्य चातिस्वरसेन निर्वाह इति । नायं पक्षः साधुः । तथा हि - भवत्येवमिह निर्वहणं तथाऽपि तत्त्वमसीत्यत्र तत्पदस्य त्वं वा अहमस्मि भगवो देवते, अहं वै त्वमसीत्यादिषु त्वंपदस्य च परदेवतावाचकत्वे त्वदुक्तनिर्वाहस्या-त्रासंभवात्। अकामेनापि तत्रास्मदुक्त निर्वाहस्य समाश्रयणे तत्समानन्यायादत्रापि तस्यैवानुसर्तुमुचितत्वादिति।

Some one has a different interpretation. The word purusha in “ *yosavasou purushah sohamasmi* ” does not refer to God but to a purified *jeeva* . Thus the statement means “One who is a purified *jeeva* , who is having the form that would be seen in *moksha* is me”. Here the word “me” fits in well with its first person usage and well communicates the unity with the person referenced as “one who is” - This interpretation is not correct. For, it may fit in well in the present context but not in other similar statements such as “ *tvam vaa ahamasmi bhagavo devate* ” and “ *aham vai tvamasi* ”. In these cases the word “ *tvam* ” speaks of God and hence an interpretation as above is not possible. If our interpretation is accepted even if reluctantly, the same rationale can be adopted in understanding these statements as well.

स्यादेतदेवं त्वं वा अहमस्मि भगवो देवते, अहं वै त्वमसीत्यत्र कथं पुरुषव्यवस्था त्वमहंशब्दयोरुभयोरपि श्रवणात्। उद्देश्यविषयकमेव युष्मदादिपदमुपपदत्वेन पाणिनिसूत्राभिप्रेतम् । यथा चोद्देश्य-समर्पकोपपदवशादेवात्र मध्यमोत्तमयोर्व्यवस्था सिध्यतीति चेत् । अस्त्वेवमिह

समाधानं तथाऽपि तत्वमसीत्यत्र पुरुषव्यवस्था न घटते तत्र सत्वंपदयोगवत्तत्पदयोगस्यापि सत्त्वात्। तथा चासीतिवदस्तीति प्रथमपुरुषस्यापि प्रसङ्गः। नह्यत्रापि त्वंपदमुद्देश्यसमर्पकम्। येन त्वंपदमेव पुरूषनिमित्तं न तु तत्पदमपीति व्यवस्था स्यात्। तथा च तत्त्वमसीतिनिरूपणावसरे भाष्यम् - नात्र किंचिदुद्दिश्य किमपि विधीयत इति। तस्मात्तत्त्वमस्तीति प्रसङ्गो दुर्वार इति। अत्रोच्यते - तत्त्वमसीत्यत्रापि त्वंपदार्थ उद्देश्य एव। ततश्चोद्देश्यविषयक-युष्मत्पदवशात्तत्र मध्यम एवेति न प्रथमपुरुषप्रसङ्गः। नच भाष्यविरोधः। भाष्यस्य विधेयांशमात्रनिषेधपरतयोद्देश्यांश-निषेधकत्वाभावात्। तथा हि - नह्येवं भाष्याभिप्रायः। नात्र किंचिदुद्दिश्यते। न च किंचिद्विधीयत इति। अपि त्वेवमभिप्रायः। त्वंपदेन किंचिदुद्दिश्यत एव किंतूद्दिष्टे तत्र न किंचिदपि विधीयत इति कथमवगम्यत इति चेत्याप्तस्यैवोपसंहारत्वोपपादकभाष्येणैव विधेयांश एव निषिध्यत इत्यभिप्रायस्य व्यक्तत्वात्।

If we are to go by the "one who is .. is me" style of interpretation, it cannot provide an answer to the specific usage of words "you" and "me" in *"tvam vaa ahamasmi* " and " *aham vai tvamasi* ", where two different persons are indicated. *Paanini sootras* on grammar say that the decision on the usage of first person, second person or third person should be based on the intended individual. The proximity of the intended person to the verb decides whether it should be considered as first, second or third person. This however would not facilitate the interpretation of unity in the statement " *tatvam asi* ". For, in the said statement the word " *tat* " also exists like " *tvam* ". Thus if " *asi* ", which is in second person were to find a place, it should have been " *asti* " as well in first person, instead. There is nothing to indicate that the relevance of verb should be only with " *tvam* " and not with " *tat* ". Sri *Ramanujacharya* in his *Sutra Bhasya* , while explaining the statement " *tatvamasi* " has said "it cannot be that something is intended and something else is spoken. Hence if unity was intended, the statement should have read as tat tvam *asti* ".It cannot be said that the word " *tvam* " is also directed towards the intended individual and hence the statement is in second person. This does not contradict the aforesaid clarification of Sri *Ramanujacharya* . Sri

Ramaanujaacharya has only criticized linking of the assignment part and not of the intended part. The clarification is only intended to link the intended and the usage of person. This is not true. In the referred statement there is nothing which is assigned nor intended. The word " *tvam* " though is an intended individual, nothing is meant to be assigned to him. That which is acquired is spelt later than the one which acquires.

अन्य आह त्वं राजाऽस्यहं राजाऽस्मीत्यादिवत्ताधीन्यादुपचारविवक्षया तत्त्वमसि सोऽहमस्मीत्यादिषु मध्यमोत्तमसामानाधिकरण्यानाम् असामञ्जस्यमिति । तदप्युपेक्षणीयमेव । लोकवेदयोश्चेतनपर्यन्तं देवमनुष्यादिव्यवहारबलेन जातिगुण-शब्दवन्मुख्यस्यैव संभव उपचारकल्पनस्यान्याय्यत्वात् ॥ १६॥

Some one else says, just like the usage "you are the king, I am the king" where the person says himself as the king, he intends only to say that he is under the control of the king, the statement " *tat tvam asi* " is also to indicate subordination to God. Even this interpretation is to be ignored. All the texts, whether authored or unauthored (*veda*), have adopted the rule of interpretation that while the primary meaning is feasible, a secondary and formal meaning should not be accepted. This is applicable where the usage is with reference to deities, men etc. Primary meaning here means, applicability of the intent of the words to a person who has the class and qualities indicated by such words. The words should not be interpreted in the secondary sense to address some one else where there is no hurdle in assigning them to the primary. Hence the secondary meaning, of some one being subordinate to God being called as God, cannot be accepted.

Madhwaachaarya : विष्णुरेकऋषिर्ज्ञेयो यमो नियमनाद्धरिः । सूर्यस्स सूरिगम्यत्वात् प्राजापत्यः प्रजापतेः । विशेषेणैव गम्यत्वादहं चासावहेयत: ।

Vishnu is *ekarshi* . He is the one who needs to be known. He is *yama* because he regulates (does *niyamana*). He is *soorya* because he is the destination for all the wise men (*soori*). He is especially the destination for *prajaapati* (*Brahma* , the creator) and hence is *praajaapatya* . He is *aham* because he is aheya (never to be discarded).

The word eka means *pradhana* (main) and *Rsh* means knowledge. Thus, *ekarshi* means the one who is the principal embodiment of knowledge. This means that God has the in-depth knowledge of everything by his very nature.

अस्मि नित्यास्तितामानात्सर्वजीवेषु संस्थितः । स्वयं तु सर्वजीवेभ्यो व्यतिरिक्तः परो हरिः । स क्रतुर्ज्ञानरूपत्वादग्निरङ्गप्रणेतृत ॥ इति ब्रह्माण्डे ।

सत्यं ब्रह्म हृदये धारयतीति सत्यधर्मा । एकोऽसौशब्द: प्राणे स्थित इति ॥१७॥

The word " *asmi* " means, He is present in all living beings at all times and is known as such. However, he is different from all beings and is superior to them all. He is called " *kratu* " because he is the embodiment of knowledge. He is also called " *agni* " because he leads *anga* (the body or the world). The entire of this (right from the commentary to mantra-15) is quoted from *BrahmaaNDa purana* .

After closing the quote, *aacharya* puts forth his explanations to the words that were not covered therein.

- He who bears satya, God in his heart is called "satyadharma" - devotee.
- There are two " *asou* " words in the above mantra. One of them means "he who dwels in *asu* , *praaNa* ". The other word means "This person (God)".
- There are two components in the word " *asmi* " viz. " *asa* " (ever present in all living beings) and " *mi* " (known).

वायुरनिलममृतम्

वायुरनिलममृतमथेदं भस्मान्तं शरीरम् ।

ॐ क्रतो स्मर कृतं स्मर क्रतो स्मर कृतं स्मर ॥ १८ ॥

vaayuranilam amritam athedam bhasma-antagm Sareeram |

Om krato smara kritam smara krato smara kritam smara |18|

Sankaraachaarya : अथेदानीं मम मरिष्यतो वायुः प्राणः अध्यात्मपरिच्छेदं हित्वा अधिदैवतात्मानं सर्वात्मकम् अनिलम् अमृतं सूत्रात्मानं प्रतिपद्यतामिति वाक्यशेषः । लिङ्गं चेदं ज्ञानकर्मसंस्कृतमुत्क्रामत्विति द्रष्टव्यम्, मार्गयाचनसामर्थ्यात् । अथ इदं शरीरमग्नौ हुतं भस्मान्तं भस्मावशेषं भूयात् ।

When I die, let the *praaNa vaayu* set out of this body and join the all pervasive divine immortal form sootra. This is indicative of the prayer for the path through which the soul cultured with knowledge and *karma phala* would leave the body. Then, let the body be burnt to ashes.

ओमिति यथोपासनम् ओम्प्रतीकात्मकत्वात्सत्यात्मकमग्न्याख्यं ब्रह्माभेदेनोच्यते । हे क्रतो सङ्कल्पात्मक स्मर यन्मम स्मर्तव्यं तस्य कालोऽयं प्रत्युपस्थितः, अतः स्मर एतावन्तं कालं भावितं कृतम् अग्ने स्मर यन्मया बाल्यप्रभृत्यनुष्ठितं कर्म तच्च स्मर । क्रतो स्मर कृतं स्मर इति पुनर्वचनमादरार्थम् ॥

Here, the word *Om* is for worshiping the one identified by that word, the one who is an embodiment of Truth, who is also called as *agni* and who is none other than *Brahma* , God. O! *krata* , the embodiment of decisions, remember all those deeds of mine that are worth remembering. It is time to remember whatever has been done till now. O! *Agne* , do remember all that *karma* I have done till now, and all that *karma* I have done ever since my childhood.

The repetitive words are to indicate the sincerity of the prayer.

Raamaanujeeya : एवं परावरतत्वविवेकं निःश्रेयससाधनभूत-भक्तियोगं तन्निष्ठस्यानुसंधेयमन्त्रविस्तार इत्यादिशास्त्रैः प्रोक्षणादिभिः समिदादिकमिव परिशुद्धस्वरुपयाथात्म्यज्ञानेन संस्मृत्वाऽऽत्महविः समर्पणीयमित्युक्तत्वादिहापि शरीरेन्द्रियादिभ्योऽतिरिक्तं स्वात्मानं प्रथमं विशोध्य तं ब्रह्मणि समर्प्य स्वाधिकारानुगुणमर्थयते -

The sacred texts say the path of progress is "Securing the knowledge of distinction between God and others and through that, *bhakti yoga,* which is a path to achieve *moksha* . Those who are in *bhakti yoga* would progress to obtain the detailed knowledge of *vedas* ". It is a practice that before offering sticks in *homa* (sacred fire) they are purified through sprinkling of water. Similarly, when *jeeva* is to be offered in God, he needs to be purified. This is done through the knowledge of the absolutely pure God. With such knowledge in the fore of mind, one should surrender to God. Similarly here, one should purify himself after understanding that he is different from the physical body and the sense organs he has, should surrender to God and obtain whatever he is eligible for.

"भोक्ता भोग्यं प्रेरितारं च मत्वा" (श्वे.उ.१।१२) इत्यादिश्रुत्यन्तर-प्रसिद्धचिदचिदीश्वरतत्त्वत्रयमिहापि द्रष्टव्यम् । वायुः विद्याकर्मानु-गुणभगवत्संकल्पवशेन तत्र तत्र गन्तृत्वाद्वा वायुः । अनेन जीवस्याणुपरिमाणत्वं परमात्माधीनत्वं च सिध्यति। वा गतिगन्धनयोरिति धातुः। निलयरहितत्वात् । क्वचिदपि व्यवस्थितत्वाभावाच्चानिलः। अमृतम्। प्रीयमाणोऽपि देहसंताने स्वयममृतं स्वरूपतो धर्मतश्चाविनाशीत्यर्थः । "अविनाशी वा अरेऽयमात्माऽनुच्छित्तिधर्मा" (बृ.उ.४।५।१४) "न विज्ञातेविपरिलोपो विद्यते" (बृ.उ.४।३।३०) न विद्यत उच्छित्तिविनाशो यस्य सोऽनुच्छित्तिर्नित्य इत्यर्थः । अनुच्छित्तिर्धर्मो यस्यासावनुच्छित्तिधर्मेति पुनर्बहुर्व्रीहिः । नित्यज्ञानवानिति भावः। आहुश्च यामुनमुनयः -

तदेवं चित्स्वभावस्य पुंसः स्वाभाविकी चितिः ।
नानापदार्थसंसर्गात्तत्तचित्तत्वमश्नुते ॥

इति। तदमृतत्वम् "अपहतपाप्मा विरजो विमृत्युः" (छा.उ.८।१५) इति श्रुतेः।

अनिलममृतमिति पुंलिङ्गत्वेन विवरणीयं वायुरिति पुंलिङ्गत्वेनोपक्रमात् । अत्र विशिष्टवृत्त्या योगतो वा परमात्मविषयत्वं न शङ्कनीयम् । नश्वरदेहस्यानन्तरवचनेन तद्व्यावृत्त्या प्रत्यगात्मपरत्वस्यैव न्याय्यत्वात् । क्षरं प्रधानममृताक्षरं हरः क्षरात्मानावीशते देव एकः (श्वे.उ. १।१०) इति श्रुतावमृतशब्दस्य जीवे प्रयोगात् । स्वभोग्यतया प्रधानं हरतीति हरो जीव इत्यर्थः । एवं प्रत्यगात्मनोऽमृतत्वमभिधाय तच्छरीरस्य मृतत्वमवश्यमित्याह - अथेदं भस्मान्तं शरीरमिति । प्रकृतादर्थादर्थान्तरविवक्षायामथशब्दः । इदं शरीरमिति विशेष्यमीश्वरशरीरव्यवच्छेदार्थम् । कर्मवश्यशरीरं भस्मान्तमित्यर्थः।

ब्रह्मादिषु प्रलीनेषु नष्टे स्थावरजङ्गमे ।
एकस्तिष्ठति सर्वात्मा स तु नारायणोऽव्ययः॥ इत्युक्तेः ।

भस्मशब्दो दाहाख्यसंस्कारपरःसन्खननादेरप्युपलक्षकः । अत्राऽऽत्मशरीरयोरमृतत्व-मृतत्वोक्त्या भेदः समर्थ्यते । रसनादिसेवया शरीरस्य नित्यत्वसंदेहोऽपाक्रियते । स्वदेहवैराग्यं कार्यमिति च सूच्यते । शीघ्र मोक्षोपाये प्रवर्तितव्यमित्यादिकं द्योत्यते ।

Swetashvatara upanishat says “One need to understand the three *tatvas* viz. One who consumes, that which is consumed and the one who enables and steers”. Similarly here, upanishat speaks of three things – *jada* (the inert material), *jeeva* and God. Let us now understand the meaning of each of the words:

vaayuh – One who moves from place to place based on his knowledge and past deeds. This proves that *jeeva* is of atomic size and that he is dependent on God. “ *va* ” means movement.

Anilam – One who does not have a place to stay. Since he is always on the move, he is *anilam* .

Amritam – Though he moves in bodies one after the other, he is himself immortal. Immortal by *swaroopa* (his core) and *dharma* (attributes). *Brihadaaranyaka upanishat* says “this one is indestructible and his qualities never meet an end”. “knowledge is never lost”. One who never meets an end. Alternatively, one does not have qualities that have an end. *Jeeva* is eternal along with his knowledge. The saints of *Yamuna* say " *jeeva* has knowledge naturally. He experiences the same as and when he comes into contact with the objects. Jeeva's immortality is vouched by *Chandogya upanishat* as well as " *apahatapaapma virajo vimrityuh* ".

Since the word vaayuh is in masculine gender, other words viz. *Anilam* , *amritam* explaining the same person should also have been in masculine gender instead of neutral gender. Since they are in different genders, it should not mean that they address God instead of jeeva. For, the very next word speaks of the mortality of his body. The said words have to be understood to explain jeeva alone and not God. We can see how in *Swetashvatara upanishat* the word *amrita* has been used with reference to jeeva in the mantra " *ksharam pradhaanam amrita-aksharam harah ksharaatmanaav-eeshate deva ekah* " - *pradhaana* (matter) is transient whereas hara is immortal and indestructible. God alone is the lord of both. Here, the word *hara* means one who takes away (*harati*), i.e., consumes matter – *jeeva* .

Idam Bhasmaantam shareeram – After thus explaining the eternity of *jeeva* , upanishat now speaks of his body as mortal. This body ends in ash. There is a word " *atha* " preceding this explanation about body. That is to indicate that the subject matter of description has changed. The word " *idam* " meaning "this", is to emphasize the aspect of mortality of these physical bodies of jeevas and not of God. These bodies of *jeevas* that are obtained consequent to their past *karma* will all end in becoming ash. So goes the script "when all these mobile and immobile entities are lost at the time when *brahma* disintegrates in God, all that is left is just Naarayana who is everything. Though the reference of "ash" is in the context of bodies being burnt after death, it should be understood to include those that are buried.

With this, it is made clear that body is different from *jeeva* , bodies are mortal, they remain as mortals even if attempted to make immortal through use of chemicals and that, one should quickly turn towards the path of salvation by discarding too much of an attachment to ones own body.

एवं चिदचिद्विवेकमुक्त्वा प्रेरितारं महापुरुषं प्रणवेनोपादत्ते - ॐमिति । उक्तं च योगानुशासने । क्लेशकर्मविपाकाशयैः अपरामृष्टः पुरुषविशेष ईश्वरः । तस्य वाचकः प्रणवः । आह च सर्वज्ञो महादेवः- "ओमित्येवं सदा विप्राः पठध्वं ध्यात केशवम्" इति द्रष्टव्यम् । यद्वा शरीरमात्मानं च विविच्य विविक्तमात्मानमोंकारवाच्ये परमपुरुषे समर्पयत्योमिति । प्रणवस्याऽऽत्मसमर्पणपरत्वमोमित्यात्मानं युञ्जीत । "प्रणवो धनुः शरो ह्यात्मा ब्रह्म तल्लक्ष्यमुच्यते । अप्रमत्तेन वेद्धव्यं शरवत्तन्मयो भवेत् । (मु० २।२।४) इत्यादिशु प्रसिद्धम् । अथ क्रतुरूपिणं विष्णुं ज्ञानयज्ञगोचरमभिमुखीकुर्वंस्तदनुग्रहं प्रार्थयते - क्रतो स्मर क्रतो ज्योतिष्टोमादिकत्वात्मक । अहं कतुरहं यज्ञ इति वचनात् । यज्ञः पञ्चमहायज्ञात्मक इत्यर्थः । स्मर स्मरणानुग्रहया बुद्ध्या विषयी कुरु ।

अहं स्मरामि मद्भक्तं नयामि परमां गतिम्। इति भगवदचनम्।

अत्र स्मरामि नयामीति पदद्वयस्य क्रतो स्मराग्ने नयेति प्रार्थनाद्वयापेक्षया प्रतिवचनत्वावगमात् । कृतं स्मर यत्कृतं यत्किंचिदानुकूल्यमनुसंधाय कृतज्ञस्त्वं मां रक्षेति वा । एतावदन्तं त्वत्कृत्यतयाऽऽनुकूल्यं प्रतिसंधाय त्वमेव शेषपूरणं कुर्विति भावः । उक्तार्थ आदरातिशयाक्रतो स्मर कृतं स्मरेत्यावृत्तिः ॥१७॥

After thus explaining the difference between *chetana* and *jada* , upanishat now explains their regulator. *Yogaanushaasana* (the book that deals with the study and practice of yoga) says "One who is untouched by difficulty, duty, ripening (mutation) and desires is eeshwara – God. Pranava (*Om*) is his name". The omniscient *Mahadeva* also has told "O! *Brahmanas* , utter *om* at all times and meditate on *keshava* ". Alternatively, the word " *om* " can be understood to mean self surrender to the supreme being God after understanding the difference between the body and *jeeva* . So says *Mundaka upanishat* " *Pranava* is the bow, *jeeva* is the arrow, *brahma* is the target. One who has a clear understanding should become the arrow and hit the target". Now, the seeker prays God, who is addressed as *kratu*. *Kratu* means *yajna* in the form of *jyotishtoma* etc and also *jnaana yajna* (the activity of serious learning of philosophy). As told in Bhagavad Geeta, God calls himself as *yajna* . Hence he is addressed as *kratu* here. He stays in the form of five *mahayajnas* (teaching is *brahma yajna* , offering to departed parents and other ancestors is *pitru yajna* , offering in sacrificial fire is *homa, bali* – spreading cooked food in the open is *bhoota yajna* and offering food to fellow humans is *nriyajna*).(अध्यापनं ब्रह्मायज्ञः पितृयज्ञस्तु तर्पणम् । होमो दैवो बलिर्भौतो नृयज्ञोतिथि पूजनम्).

Thus the statement is "O! *Krato* , do remember me, remember me for whatever I have done.

This remembrance is for bestowing benefits on me. So says God "I remember my devotee and take him to *moksha* ". Remember me for whatever good I have done and in gratitude, protect me. Please fill the gaps in my performance for the purpose.

A repetition of the expression is to show the seriousness attached to the prayer.

<u>Madhwaachaarya</u> : यस्मिन्नयं स्थितः सोऽप्यमृतः किमु परः। अः ब्रह्मैव निलयनं यस्य वायोः सोऽनिलम् । "अतिरोहितविज्ञानाद्वायुरप्यमृतः स्मृतः । मुख्यामृतः स्वयं रामः परमात्मा सनातनः" इति रामसंहितायाम् ॥१८॥

When the one who is staying in God is himself immortal, what to say that God is immortal. With this message, the word *anila* is used as an adjective to *vaayu* , the deity in charge of life. The word *anila* literally means the one who has " *a* " (God) as his residence. It is generally understood that only God and godess Laxmi are immortal and all others have to face separation from their body. How then, *vaayu* is referred to as immortal here. In answer, the Acharya quotes from " *Raama Samhita* " as under:

"Since *vaayu* retains his knowledge and awareness at all times, he is also considered as immortal. The absolute immortal is *Rama* , the God himself, who is eternal".

Thus, this mantra emphasizes on the eternal nature of God even though he dwells in mortal bodies of others. The mortal bodies of us and other living beings meet an end on some day. But *vaayu* and God remain unaffected with the same.

"भक्तानां स्मरणं विष्णोःर्नित्यज्ञप्तिस्वरूपतः । अनुग्रहोन्मुखत्वं तु नैवान्यत्क्वचिदिष्यते" इति ब्रह्मतर्के । ॥१८॥

Vishnu knows and remembers everything at all times. Hence the prayer for remembrance is only to make him look at the seeker for showering the benefits and not that he has forgotten.

अग्ने नय सुपथा राये

अग्ने नय सुपथा राये अस्मान्विश्वानि देव वयुनानि विद्वान् ।
युयोध्यस्मज्जुहुराणमेनो भूयिष्ठां ते नमउक्तिं विधेम ॥ १९ ॥

agne naya supathaa raaye asmaan

viShvaani deva vayunaani vidvaan |

yuyodhyasmaat juhuraaNameno

bhooyiShtaam te nama uktim vidhema |19|

Sankaraachaarya : पुनरन्येन मन्त्रेण मार्गं याचते -

हे अग्ने नय गमय सुपथा शोभनेन मार्गेण । सुपथेति विशेषणं दक्षिणमार्गनिवृत्त्यर्थम् । निर्विण्णोऽहं दक्षिणेन मार्गेण गतागतलक्षणेन ; अतो याचे त्वां पुनः पुनः गमनागमनवर्जितेन शोभनेन पथा नय । राये धनाय, कर्मफलभोगायेत्यर्थः । अस्मान् यथोक्तधर्मफलविशिष्टान् विश्वानि सर्वाणि हे देव वयुनानि कर्माणि, प्रज्ञानानि वा विद्वान् जानन् ।

The seeker prays for the path through another *mantra* .

O! *Agni* , take me through the fair path. The word "fair" is used to indicate exclusion of the southern path. "I am tired of the southern path that is characterized by its returnable nature. Hence, I beg you again and again to take me through fair path that does not put me back in to this cycle of coming and going". Having known all those pious deeds, that are linked to specified fruits, performed by me and knowledge gained (progress in the path of knowledge made) by me, do take me in the proper path to facilitate enjoyment of the fruits of *karma* .

किञ्च, युयोधि वियोजय विनाशय अस्मत् अस्मत्तः जुहुराणं कुटिलं वञ्चनात्मकम् एनः पापम् । ततो वयं विशुद्धाः सन्तः इष्टं प्राप्स्याम इत्यभिप्रायः । किन्तु वयमिदानीं ते न शक्नुमः परिचर्यां कर्तुम् ; भूयिष्ठां बहुतरां ते तुभ्यं नमउक्तिं नमस्कारवचनं विधेम नमस्कारेण परिचरेम इत्यर्थः ॥

Further, please distance us from the cunning verbal sins. With that, having purified ourselves, we will attain the desired (*moksha*). However we are not able to serve you. We offer you plenty of salutations. We serve you through these salutations.

“अविद्यया मृत्युं तीर्त्वा विद्ययामृतमश्नुते” (ई. उ. ११) “विनाशेन मृत्युं तीर्त्वा असम्भूत्यामृतमश्नुते” (ई. उ. १४) इति श्रुत्वा केचित्संशयं कुर्वन्ति । अतस्तन्निर्धारणार्थं सङ्क्षेपतो विचारणां करिष्यामः।

On hearing the texts “after surpassing the death with *vidya* , one attains salvation through *avidya* ” and “after surpassing death with destruction, one achieves salvation through creation”, a few get confused. Hence we will discuss it in brief hereunder.

तत्र तावत्किंनिमित्तः संशय इति, उच्यते -

Now what is causing the confusion?

विद्याशब्देन मुख्या परमात्मविद्यैव कस्मान्न गृह्यते, अमृतत्वं च ?

Why is “ *vidya* ” not understood to mean the knowledge of the supreme God and “ *amrita* ”, the Salvation?

ननूक्तायाः परमात्मविद्यायाः कर्मणश्च विरोधात्समुच्चयानुपपत्तिः ।

Since the purports of *paramaatma vidya* (Knowledge of supreme God) and of *karma* (path of performance) are contradictory, does it then mean they cannot be counted as complementary nature?

सत्यम् । विरोधस्तु नावगम्यते, विरोधाविरोधयोः शास्त्रप्रमाणकत्वात् । यथा अविद्यानुष्ठानं विद्योपासनं च शास्त्रप्रमाणकम् , तथा तद्विरोधाविरोधावपि । यथा च “न हिंस्यात्सर्वा भूतानि” इति शास्त्रादवगतं पुनः शास्त्रेणैव बाध्यते “अध्वरे पशुं हिंस्यात्” इति । एवं विद्याविद्ययोरपि स्यात् विद्याकर्मणोश्च समुच्चयः ।

True. But the contradiction is not perceived here. Any contradiction can be only based on supportive evidence from scripts. Just the way practicing *vidya* and adopting *avidya* are scripturally authentic, even their contradiction or otherwise (are also authentic). An example of the kind is where the scriptures mandate that there shall be no cruelty towards animals but then contradict by prescribing animal sacrifice in the *yajna* . Similar is the case with *vidya* and *avidya* . So is the case of the co-existance of *vidya* and *karma*.

न ; "दूरमेते विपरीते विषूची अविद्या या च विद्येति ज्ञाता" (क. उ. १ । २ । ४) इति श्रुतेः ।

Nay. The aforesaid exception cannot be applied here. The scriptures aver that *vidya* and *avidya* are different and opposite in meaning.

विद्यां चाविद्यां च इति वचनादविरोध इति चेत् न हेतुस्वरूपफलविरोधात् ।

If it is to be said that there is no contradiction citing the very words of upanishat viz. " *vidyaam cha avidyaam cha* " etc, it is not true. They are different by their nature and by the benefits they bestow.

विद्याविद्याविरोधाविरोधयोर्विकल्पासम्भवात् समुच्चयविधानात् अविरोध एवेति चेत् न सहसम्भवानुपपत्तेः । क्रमेणैकाश्रये स्यातां विद्याविद्ये इति चेत् , न ; विद्योत्पत्तौ तदाश्रयेऽविद्यानुपपत्तेः

Since *vidya* and *avidya* cannot be had as contradictory to each other and also as non-contradictory, they can only be treated as complementary on account of them being told together. Is not it? No, they cannot exist at the same place. Why not? vidya and avidya can exist at the same place one after the other. Is not it? No. with the onset of vidya, the avidya extinguishes. Hence there is no question of both of them staying in the same location.

न हि अग्निरुष्णः प्रकाशश्च इति विज्ञानोत्पत्तौ यस्मिन्नाश्रये तदुत्पन्नम् , तस्मिन्नेवाश्रये शीतोऽग्निरप्रकाशो वा इत्यविद्याया उत्पत्तिः । नापि संशयः अज्ञानं वा, "यस्मिन्सर्वाणि भूतानि

आत्मैवाभूद्विजानतः । तत्र को मोहः कः शोक एकत्वमनुपश्यतः" (ई. उ. ७) इति शोकमोहाद्यसम्भवश्रुतेः। अविद्यासम्भवात्तदुपादानस्य कर्मणोऽप्यनुपपत्तिमवोचाम।

When one gets to know that the fire is characterized by heat and light, the knowledge (*vidya*) of fire is born in him. It is not possible for the same person to get *avidya* of fire which would have meant fire to be cold and lacklustre. Similarly when *vidya* sets in, there is neither *avidya* nor any doubt. The vedic text " *yasmin sarvaani...ekatvamanupasyatah* " confirms that there is neither pain nor illusion with the onset of knowledge. Since there is no room for avidya, we say that even *karma* , the outcome of *avidya* also ceases to exist.

"अमृतमश्नुते" इत्यापेक्षिकममृतम् । विद्याशब्देन परमात्मविद्याग्रहणे "हिरण्मयेन" (ई. उ. १५) इत्यादिना द्वारमार्गयाचनमनुपपन्नं स्यात्। तस्मात् यथाव्याख्यात एव मन्त्राणामर्थ इत्युपरम्यते॥

" *amritamasnute* " - *amritam* , the salvation is the most sought after thing. If we interpret *vidya* as the knowledge of supreme God, the appeal for opening the path through " *hiranmayena* .." etc. will not be relevant. Hence, we conclude that our interpretation that *vidya* does not refer to *paramaatma vidyaa,* the specialized knowledge of the supreme God is apt for the mantra.

इति श्रीमत्परमहंसपरिव्राजकाचार्यस्य
श्रीगोविन्दभगवत्पूज्यपादशिष्यस्य श्रीमच्छङ्करभगवतः
कृतौ ईशावास्योपनिषद्भाष्यम् सम्पूर्णम्॥

***

Raamaanujeeya : बृहदारण्यके पञ्चमेऽध्याये यदा वै पुरुषोऽस्माल्लोकात्प्रैति स वायुमागच्छति (बृ.उ. १०।१) इत्यादिनाऽर्चिरादिकं पन्थानमुपदिश्य पश्चादध्यायावसाने हिरण्मयेन पात्रेणेत्याद्याश्चत्वारो मन्त्राः क्रमेण पठिताः । अग्नेऽग्निशरीरक "यस्याग्निः शरीरम्" इति श्रुतेः । यद्वा साक्षादप्यविरोधं जैमिनिः (ब्र.सू. १।२।२८) अग्रं नयतीत्यग्निः । अग्रनयनादिगुणयुक्त नय प्रवर्तयेत्यर्थः। सुपथा शोभनेन मार्गेणाचिरादिना।

अर्चिरहःसितपक्षानुदगयनाब्दौ च मारुतार्केन्दून्।
अपि वैद्युतवरुणेन्द्रप्रजापतीनातिवाहिकानाहुः (वरदमिश्रः)॥

इत्यभियुक्तसंगृहीतेन मार्गेणेति भावः। राये धनाय ब्रह्मणः प्राप्यत्वाद्ब्रह्मैव सुस्थिरमनन्तधनं तस्मै हिरण्मयपुरुषाय त्वत्प्राप्तय इति भावः। अस्माननन्यप्रयोजनात्। अनन्यगतींश्चेत्यर्थः। न केवलं मामपि त्वनुबन्धिजनानपीति बहुवचनस्याभिप्राय:। देव मम बुद्धौ द्योतमान। तं ह देवमात्मबुद्धिप्रकाशं मुमुक्षुर्वै शरणमहं प्रपद्ये। (श्वे.उ.६।१८) इति श्रुतेः। विश्वानि वयुनानि। चतुर्विधपुरुषार्थो-पायान्यथावद्विद्वांस्त्वमस्मान्नेतुमर्हसीति भावः। "यो वै वेदांश्च प्रहिणोति तस्मै, (श्वे.उ.६।१८) इति श्रुतेरिति भावः। मुमुक्षुर्वै शरणमहं प्रपद्य इति मन्त्रगतं मुमुक्षुपदं विवृण्वन्नाह - युयोध्यस्मज्जुहुराणमेन इति हुर्छा कौटिल्ये जुहुराणं कुटिलं बन्धात्मकमित्यर्थः। एनः। अकृत्यकरणकृत्याकरणादिरूपं त्वदुपासनो-त्पत्तिप्रतिबन्धमित्यर्थः। त्वत्प्राप्तिप्रतिबन्धकमिति वा। एन इति जात्यभिप्रायकम्। अस्मदस्मत्तः। युयोधि पृथक्कुरु।

In the fifth *adhyaaya* of *Brihadaaranyaka upanishat,* the path of travel to *moksha* is described. On leaving the last physical body, *jeeva* travels to *vaayu loka* etc. In the last part of it, we have four mantras beginning with " *hiranmayena paatrena* ". It is this path that is referred to here, in the present *mantra* .

This *mantra* is in the form of a prayer. Let us examine the meaning of the words in it.

Agne – O! *Agni* . One who has fire as his body. *Veda* says " *yasya agnih shareeram* ". The word also can mean the deity of fire as explained in *Brahma sutra* 1-2-28. The literal meaning of *Agni* , is the one who leads from the front.

Naya – Take

Asmaan - us. We have no other benefit to seek and no one to depend on. It is not just me who needs to be taken but all those who are following me. Hence the plural usage.

Supathaa - in the flawless path. The flawless path to moksha is called " *archiraadi maarga* " - one where the first station is " *archir loka* " world by name " *archis* ". *Varada Mishra* describes the path as having the following stations in the same order: *archir -> ahah -> shukla paksha -> uttaraayana -> samvatsara -> marut -> arka -> indu -> vidyut -> varuna -> indra -> prajaapati -> aativaahika* .

Raaye – for securing the wealth. Since the destiny is *Brahma* , wealth here means the infinite and everlasting wealth in the form of *Brahma* .

Deva – O! One who is visible in my mind. *Swetashvatara upanishat* has such an usage " *tam ha vai devam aatmabuddhi-prakaasham...* "*Vidwan* – the one who knows the means to achieve (*Swetashvatara upanishat* quotes him as the one who provides even *vedas*)

Vishwaani vayunaani – all the four types of *purushaartha* – desirables (*dharma, artha, kaama, moksha*).

Yuyodhi – separate (the meaning of the word *mumukshu* as intended in the later part of the quoted *Swetashvatara upanishat* is taken here). Take us away from the cause of cycle of births and deaths.

Juhuraanam – the one that is causing bondage to the cycle of births and deaths.

Enam – and the set of actions involving doing of prohibited and not doing the prescribed, thereby preventing *upaasana* of God and causing an obstacle in achieving *moksha* .

Asmat – from us.

एतावदेव याचे त्वां जुहुराणमेनोऽस्मत्तः प्रथमं वियोजयेति तत्पश्चाद्यथामनोरथं विनाशय पुरुषान्तरे संक्रामय वा न तत्रास्माकं निर्बन्ध इति भावः । भूयिष्ठाम् । अनन्यगतित्वेनाऽऽवृत्तितो भूयसीम् । नमउक्तिं । ते । आप्तकामतया निरुपाधिकस्वामितया च नमउक्तिम् । निरपेक्षाय ते विधेम विधमहे

। हेऽग्ने देव विश्वानि वयुनानि विद्वांस्त्वं जुहुराणमेनोऽस्मत्तो युयोधि सुपथाऽस्मान्राये नय वयं ते भूयिष्ठां नमउक्तिं विधेमेत्यन्वयः । नित्याञ्जलिपुटा हृष्टा नम इत्येवंवादिनो भवाम इति भावः ॥ १८ ॥

I pray only this that you do distance us from those causing births and deaths. Beyond this, you do whatever you feel like – destroy me, merge me with some one or whatsoever. I do not have an objection for it. Since you are the only one I believe in, I bow aplenty to you, the one who have no unfulfilled desire and you are an unqualified lord of me. My salutes to you, who does not expect anything from me.

To summarize - O! *Agni, deva* , you know everything that would bestow the desired benefits. Isolate us from the aspects that tie us to this world and lead us in the flawless path to *moksha* . We salute you in abundance. We stay at all times with our hands joined like a bowl and a blissful heart and say " *namah* " to you.

एवमस्मिन्नध्याय आदितो मन्त्राष्टकस्य तु परतत्त्वं ततो मन्त्राटकस्य परमपुरुषविषयकं भक्तियोगरूपं साक्षात्साधनमवशिष्टमन्त्रद्विकस्य सर्वफलसाधनप्रपदनं प्रधानप्रतिपाद्यम् । एवं च भगवद्गीताध्यायषट्कं प्रथमं प्रथमाष्टकस्योपबृहणं द्वितीयषट्कमुपरितनाष्टकस्य चरमश्लोकस्य पूर्वार्धं वायुरनिलममृतमन्त्रोक्तानुष्ठानविधायकमुत्तरार्धं तु युयोध्यस्मज्जुहुराणमेन इति प्रार्थयमानानां प्रार्थनापूरणसंकल्प-पूर्वकं शोकप्रतिक्षेपकं चरमश्लोकोऽप्यस्य मन्त्रद्विकस्योपबृंहणमिति बोध्यम् ।

Thus, the first eight *mantras* of this upanishat spoke of God, the next eight *mantras* spoke of devotion towards the supreme God as a means and the balance of two mantras (mantras numbered 16 and 17 are considered as one) spoke of the highest of benefits that anybody would desire. The first six *adhyaayas* of Bhagavat Geeta is like an explanation of the first eight *mantras* of this upanishat. The next six *adhyaayas* of Bhagavat Geeta elaborate the contents of the second set of eight *mantras* of this upanishat.

The first half of the last *sloka* of the twelfth *adhyaaya* of Bhagavat Geeta communicates the meaning of the 18th mantra i.e, *anushthaana* (the practice) and its later half of the result of prayer.

इति रामानुजमतानुयायिनारायणकृत
प्रकाशिकासमतेशावास्योपनिषत् ।

***

<u>Madhwaachaarya</u> : वयुनं ज्ञानम् "त्वद्दत्तया वयुनयेदमचष्ट विश्वम्" इति वचनात् । जुहुराणं अस्मान् अल्पीकुर्वत् । युयोधि वियोजय । यदस्मान्कुरुतेऽत्यल्पांस्तदेनोऽस्मद्वियोजय । नय नो मोक्षवित्तायेत्यस्तौद्यज्ञमनु । इति स्कान्दे । युयु वियोग इति धातुः । भक्तिज्ञानाभ्यां भूयिष्ठां नमउक्ति विधेम ॥२०॥"

Vayunam " means knowledge. There is an usage of the kind to indicate this meaning for *vayuna* – (*tvad dattayaa vayunayaa idam aachashta vishvam* - Understand this world with the knowledge given by you). The word " *juhuraanam* " means belittling. " *yuyodhi* " means isolate. Sri *Aacharya* quotes from *skaanda puraaNa* as under:

Manu prayed that form of God whose name is *yajna* as follows: "Please isolate us from whatever that would belittle us. Lead us to the wealth of salvation".

We prostrate to you profusely with devotion and knowledge.

Acharya concludes with his prayer:

पूर्णशक्तिचिदानन्दश्रीतेज:स्पष्टमूर्तये ।
ममाभ्यधिकमित्राय नमो नारायणाय ते ॥

Salutations to *naaraayaNa* who is the complete embodiment of power, knowledge, bliss, wealth, and energy and who is my closest friend.

इति श्रीमदानन्दतीर्थभगवत्पादाचार्यविरचितं

ईशावास्योपनिषद्भाष्यं समाप्तम् ॥

***

**** ॥ श्रीकृष्णार्पणमस्तु ॥ ****

www.ingramcontent.com/pod-product-compliance
Lightning Source LLC
LaVergne TN
LVHW100335181026
850499LV00039B/1082